WOW! WORDS

Building Children's Powerful Oral Vocabularies (Ages 4–7)

by Babs Bell Hajdusiewicz

♥ GOOD YEAR BOOKS

Dedication

Thank you to my treasured educator friends—Gail Blasser Riley, Linda Lott, Sylvia Harvey, Mary Ann Chapman, the late Mary Carter Smith, Meg Green, Eliah Perez, and others far too numerous to mention—for their ongoing support and encouragement in my determination to bring to print this body of work that shares decades of my observations of children's successes with *WOW! Words.* Special thanks to my editor, Bobbie Dempsey, and to Helen and Howard Fisher, for their unending patience and belief in me and my passion for time spent with children, teachers, and parents.

❤ GOOD YEAR BOOKS

Our titles are available for most basic curriculum subjects plus many enrichment areas. For information on other Good Year Books and to place orders, contact your local bookseller or educational dealer, or visit our website at www.goodyearbooks.com. For a complete catalog, please contact:

Good Year Books
A division of Social Studies School Service
10200 Jefferson Boulevard
Culver City, California 90232-0802
www.goodyearbooks.com

Contributing Writer: Sydnie Meltzer Kleinhenz
Copy Editor: Mindy Poder
Proofreader: Justin Coffey
Musicians: Donald Milton III and Travis Vaughn III

Cover Design and Illustrations: Gabriela Fleming
Text Design: Doug Goewey
Art Credits: From istockphoto.com: dripping faucet illustration, p. 68, © Kevin Green; cell phone illustration, p. 69, © Jayesh Bhagat; girl singing illustration, p. 94, © micha archer; binoculars illustration, p. 145, © robodread; mirror illustration, p. 160, © grimgram
By A.R. Harter: boy and dog illustration, p. 61; activities illustration, p. 112; reluctant girl illustration, p. 118; ball in storm drain illustration, p. 126

ISBN-10: 1-59647-070-4
ISBN-13: 978-1-59647-070-5

PREFACE

Melanie's hand shot up at the sound from the wall speaker. She knew our principal's first words of greeting would be: "Good morning! I have some special announcements...." Still, Melanie waited patiently till the principal had finished.

"I know! I know!" she bubbled. "He *could* say 'specific' announcements." Then she added, "I was really patient, right?"

"Me, too!" said Wade. "I was patient. I have to go to the bathroom."

The school day had barely begun. Yet, Melanie had already used two WOW! Words™ in correct contexts. And Wade *had* wowed us in more ways than one. Not only had he used a big word; he had waited patiently. Weeks earlier, I had chosen to introduce that particular WOW! Word in hopes it might motivate Wade and some others to improve on a behavior or two. Indeed, my students talked confidently. However, when presented with pencil-and-paper tasks, these ten- to fourteen-year-old talkers struggled with skills expected of first graders. They owned WOW! Words, though, and they sought every opportunity to talk using those big words.

Focusing on Oral Language

This book is about the oral language learning of thousands of toddlers to teens—some like Melanie and Wade, others with average to gifted abilities—whose talking prowess with big words could be directly traced to the use of WOW! Words, an approach to vocabulary learning that practices intentional oral modeling of big words.

WOW! Words: Building Children's Powerful Oral Vocabularies (Ages 4–7) presents child- and time-tested tools for building children's speaking vocabularies such that listeners listen up... and invariably exclaim, "Wow!" Focusing totally on oral language—listening and speaking—*WOW! Words* invites every child to be a winner, regardless of natural ability or learned skills. The goal of this book is to explain the rationale for using WOW! Words and to present instruction in the form of daily lessons for teachers, parents, and caregivers who spend time with children ages 4 though 7.

Inviting Every Child to Win

WOW! Words presents vocabulary learning that works to level the playing field for all children. It's about developing powerful speakers, regardless of children's abilities or their proficiencies in listening and speaking or reading and writing. Unlike customary vocabulary lessons and their accompanying assessments, the vocabulary learning presented in this book invites every child to experience success in hearing and saying carefully selected big words used in meaningful and useful contexts. *WOW! Words* is about building children's confidence to proudly use big words in correct contexts to express themselves orally. It's about engaging children in conversations, in school and at home—conversations that model big words in ways that invite children to adopt those words. Additionally, and very importantly, this book is about inspiring and facilitating every child's daily use of powerful vocabulary with all the ease and self-confidence of a professional. And this book is about you and how you can become a catalyst for change in the lives of children—to assist children toward learning language and toward feeling good about themselves while becoming the most powerful and confident speakers they can be.

Discovering Children's Need for Vocabulary

WOW! Words has been time-tested, allowing numerous opportunities to observe as children incorporate WOW! Words into daily activities. Although my interests in such language learning likely took root in my own childhood when my grandfather told me stories and rhymes, it was during practicum classes in undergraduate school that I focused on how children learn language. My eagerness for teaching grew with each new assignment that took me into real classrooms to learn from real teachers and real kids using ideas and strategies I'd only read about in books. I observed children succeeding, or not, in vocabulary and spelling drills. I watched as some kids read and wrote with ease, while others struggled with basic words. And I noted how children's classroom performances frequently framed how they connected with their peers, inside and outside the classroom.

During practicums, I'd teach prescribed lessons, and sometimes I gained permission to try out an original idea. Some worked well; other ideas needed more polish in their content and/or presentation. After all, I was learning how to teach. Interestingly, though, these hours of practice would mark the onset of a teaching philosophy—one that I would spend an entire career nourishing and developing—around core beliefs that children's foundational need for vocabulary, and the knowledge embedded in vocabulary, could be presented in an enticing way so that every child becomes a winner.

Seeking Ways to Reach and Teach

Some days, reality set in—such as when a supervisor suggested I work with a group of second graders in math. After reading the textbook and teacher guide, I knew what to do. But nothing worked with these kids, who were not just struggling in math but who were also struggling in reading and almost every other subject. Rampant misbehaviors added challenge. I remember thinking that perhaps my lofty goals were just that. For these kids, learning wasn't going to happen "by the book." I'd felt confident teaching language arts lessons. So far, my studies and experiences had shown me that children needed word familiarity and the knowledge that came with words. To this day, I point out to teachers and parents what a listener or reader gets from every word, even *a, an,* or *the*—little words that suggest a noun or naming word is likely coming next. My studies had taught me that success in the content areas (and on

tests) relies heavily on a child's being able to read and write basic vocabulary *and* subject-specific vocabulary.

So there I was, asked to teach second graders who had little interest in math or much else that had to do with school and learning. Searching for wisdom, I studied these children. I looked over their test scores. I listened to how they talked. I noticed how they looked at my feet when we talked. Using the teacher's guide for math, I planned a lesson for these kids. And though my lesson scarcely resembled the guide, I felt desperate. These kids needed to learn, and they needed to be able to look me in the eye.

Teaching Math…and Vocabulary… and a Whole Lot More

What happened next set the stage for other new beginnings. One lesson plan became three as these students showed keen interest and asked for more. We spent time scouring the building and grounds, looking for and naming geometric shapes. We created shapes with similar properties. We named and counted each shape's corners and sides. As soon as these children understood basic concepts, I slipped in some big-talking words—meaningful and useful vocabulary words that children might speak in correct context but not be expected to read nor write—these particular words were some that I'd learned in a high school geometry class only a few years earlier. Now, corners were sometimes called *angles,* further classified as *inside* or *outside* corners, and then labeled *acute, obtuse,* or *straight.* These second graders grabbed onto these big-talking words and asked for more. They led the way to measure line *segments,* which soon became further classified as being *parallel* or *non-parallel.* Although my lessons showed but a tinge of resemblance to the math guide, these kids were learning math and much more. Their talking vocabularies had grown exponentially. And, interestingly, they now looked me squarely in the eye when they talked, proudly using all that new vocabulary.

My supervisor shared my excitement and encouraged me to "stretch my wings," while reminding me that the students would be tested over the school's adopted curriculum. I heard the expectation. I wanted to please, and I wanted to graduate with good grades. I also wanted to make a difference in these kids' learning lives. I planned more lessons, carefully sculpting each to include the prescribed curriculum, along with ways I'd hope to incorporate the fun of geometry and big words. I tucked in notes about new big math words I might add. That term ended on a high note, both for my students—who now approached learning (and test taking) with greater interest and confidence—and for me.

Intentional Oral Modeling

During my student teaching the next semester, I found another opportunity to try out my intentional oral modeling approach, this time with three fourth-grade boys who barely recognized basic sight words. As with the second graders, these kids' failures in language arts subjects had led to failures in word-heavy social studies, science, and health classes as well. I noticed how math sometimes presented a glimmer of hope for them, until story problems required reading skills. And I'd noted the boys seemed to own limited speaking vocabularies. These ten-year-olds with average abilities were breathing in failure and breathing out hopelessness. Something positive needed to happen.

I began to model the use of a really big word in conversation each week. I used the word and some of its forms in all sorts of meaningful and useful ways—orally. After introducing a word, such as *official,* I'd toss out a challenge: "So, Fellows, who's going to *officiate* next week when I'm not here?" After more weeks and more big words, I'd announce, "Someone's being a real *curmudgeon* today!" To help the boys retain and use all the big words, along with the ideas from the many read-alouds I'd shared, I'd pose questions like, "Who feels *empowered* with *fortitude* like Hercules today?" Never did I ask these boys to read or write those big words. We just talked "big!" The bigger the talk during our conversations, the bigger the words those boys used in stories they told as I wrote—

and the wider grew their smiles of enjoyment and self-satisfaction! Our little project lasted for several weeks, but it was quickly evident that all four of us were winners. As with the second graders, these fourth-grade boys now looked me in the eye when we conversed. They talked with greater confidence than ever before. They interacted more confidently—and less combatively—with classmates. *They* knew how to use big words. And when they talked, their classmates (and teacher) exclaimed, "Wow!" Soon, the entire class joined us to hear and then say those "big-talking words," as students began to call them.

Watching Children "Dance" to Learn

Students thrived in this "oral language dance," our unique listening and speaking experience with language where every child, regardless of academic performance, could participate and come away filled with success and confidence. Children knew they were successful speakers when their listeners paid them respectful attention. And, without fail, their listeners exclaimed, "WOW!" Thus, the name "WOW! Words" seemed well-suited for this new and exciting experience with oral language. As an acronym, "WOW" aptly described this vocabulary-learning approach that focused on each big word's introduction: It was, indeed, our *Word Of the Week.* Each successive year's use with a new group of talkers brought with it new insights. I learned to select big words that were not only useful and meaningful for children but also presented challenges. After all, nary a listener is likely to say, "Wow!" upon hearing a seven-year-old tell how a ride at the amusement park was *awesome*. On the other hand, hearing a two- or three-year-old's correct use of *awesome* would grab any listener's ear as being just that: Awesome!

WOW! Words lessons became routine now. On each Monday, without any real fanfare, I'd converse with my students and casually introduce that week's new word. I'd then use that word and its forms in varying contexts every day that week. Where applicable, I'd set up activities and work areas that focused on a WOW! Word. I'd point out a word's use or show pictures illustrating its meaning. And I'd invite my students to do some "eavesdropping" homework and report any overheard uses of a WOW! Word. Some students needed my help to include the word in conversation, as the goal was, indeed, for every child to feel totally comfortable participating in this oral language dance. The next Monday, I'd similarly introduce a new big word, while continuing to make conversation and plan activities around the previous week's word. Focusing on one new WOW! Word for an entire week proved especially fruitful, because time allowed students to hear and use the word in various contexts. It also allowed children to try that word in all sorts of settings—the classroom, lunchroom, and playground and at home with family members.

Assessing Growth and Involving Families

I soon began sending home information about WOW! Words, emphasizing our oral focus. I didn't want any well-meaning family member to expect a child to read or write a WOW! Word. Family members reported they liked how homework around a WOW! Word could be completed easily while on the go. And in some homes, each new word meant more conversation took place—increasing interest and literacy success for all family members.

Weeks passed, and big words piled up—orally, that is. Assessment was easy: I just needed to listen to my students talk. Record keeping was similarly easy. At first, I merely recorded the WOW! Words on our classroom calendar, but each year's use brought new ideas. One year, children's oral dancing with WOW! Words gained a "look." By

the end of the year, we had built a caterpillar character across our classroom's wall, adding a new segment for each week's WOW! Word. Another year, children asked to *write* each new WOW! Word on its segment. Still another class's enthusiasm for WOW! Words invited talkers and listeners to mark a dot on a word's segment for each time children heard or used that WOW! Word.

Teachers and parents attending my seminars and staff-development trainings have incorporated WOW! Words into their daily living with children in classrooms and homes. A kindergarten teacher received "WOW!" exclamations from colleagues (and me) when she reported her success with intentional oral modeling of WOW! Words. She told how she'd asked her student why he looked so sad and that he had replied, "I'm full of contrition. I promised, but I forgot." Indeed, WOW! Words has been instrumental in developing impressive speaking vocabularies for many children, including my own.

Children's powerful speaking successes are at the core of my sharing *WOW! Words: Building Children's Powerful Oral Vocabularies (Ages 4–7)*. In addition, this book is a response to hundreds of requests from teachers and parents wanting hands-on tools to put WOW! Words on children's tongues during the critically important early years of children's language development. It also represents the fulfillment of my long-held career goal—to partner with those of you who seek to invite every young child to participate in an oral vocabulary experience that offers success and self-confidence, both as a learner and as a powerful speaker who never fails to capture a listener's attention in a positive way.

CONTENTS

WOW! Words for 4-year-olds

WOW! Words for 5-year-olds

WOW! Words for 6-year-olds

WOW! Words for 7-year-olds

Blackline Masters

Resources

Books and Collections

Poems and Songs by Babs Bell Hajdusiewicz and Others

Tongue Twisters

Indexes

INTRODUCTION

My friend couldn't wait to tell me what her niece had said. It seems that little Rosa had declined my friend's offer of a sandwich but had then run back to ask for "just a portion." My friend told of her surprise and one-word exclamation: "Wow!" She quickly added that Rosa had hugged her and grinned widely. And knowing about my work with children, my friend posed: "Rosa's not even four yet! Is that normal—you know, a big word like that?" No, not in my experience. In fact, I hear such big-word usage from a child Rosa's age only when and if family members or teachers have used those words in conversation with children.

Studies in early childhood language acquisition by Cullinan (1987), Hart & Risley (1995, 1999), Roskos, Tabors, and Lenhart (2009), and others support my friend's experience and my own. *WOW! Words: Building Children's Powerful Oral Vocabularies (Ages 4–7)* presents tools and resources to enable families and teachers to engage young children in rich conversation. Such conversation builds powerful oral vocabularies and spurs children's interest in learning while boosting their self-esteem when they notice that their listeners pay attention.

Engaging Children in Conversation

Oral language—listening and speaking—is where language begins. Good first teaching of oral language works systematically—sound by sound and word by word—to engage children in a kind of oral language "dance," a conversational interaction that ensures children's success as listeners and speakers and later as readers and writers.

Ideally, family members begin this oral language dance and put good first teaching into action the moment a child is born. They *talk* to the child. Engaging babies in the back-and-forth of conversational talk is, generally, a natural occurrence—an oral language interaction adults do with children. It's also how we model for children how to talk and listen. Family members talk,

listen, and talk again to present sounds and words. Listening models how one waits, giving another person time to hear and, hopefully, to respond.

Talkers begin oral language interaction when they talk to babies with the expectation that children will hear and eventually repeat those sounds and words. Obviously, good first teaching of oral language is not hard. It's not new. It's not costly. It makes sense. And it works. Children come away speaking the language or dialect they have heard used around them. They speak the words, the sayings, and the ideas and beliefs they've heard spoken in conversation with, or in proximity to, their family members and within their wider communities. And children's speech frequently reflects the very intonations and body language that seem to go with all that talk they've experienced. Ideally, babies and toddlers gain many such opportunities to listen to and practice speaking their language.

Oral Language Prepares Children to Meet Print

While good first language teaching immerses infants and very young children in the sounds of language, no one expects reading nor writing from babies and toddlers. Two-year-old Isaac is just beginning to make sense of the sound of the word that names him. Given *time* to hear his name again and again, he begins to say it in a way that others understand his intent. And soon, Isaac shows interest in learning to read and write his name.

So it goes with children's language learning, from oral language learning to calling on that foundation of listening and speaking experiences to attach those heard sounds to printed symbols. This foundation in oral language experiences builds children's confidence to read and write letters and words that, like talking, hold meaning. Indeed, engaging children in the listening and speaking interactions provided by conversation sets the stage for boundless eagerness to read and write.

As children's families and communities vary, however, so do their experiences with listening and speaking. Thus, children bring to school a wide range of oral language experiences. While some children come armed with confidence coupled with bountiful eagerness to read and write, other children lack the conversation skills that result in confidence around meeting print.

Children Learn to Talk

It's no secret that children seek out and thrive on attention. Research and practice point out a wide and noticeable difference and importance in the amount of positive attention children may encounter in their daily lives. Summarizing their longitudinal studies in homes of young children, Hart & Risley (1999, 170) share this startling contrast: "Some 4-year-old children would have heard more than 800,000 affirmatives from their parents, [such as "I like what you did," or "Good."], whereas others would have heard fewer than 80,000. The differences in the children's test scores on the PPVT-R [Peabody Picture Vocabulary Test-Revised] and the TOLD-2 [Test of Language Development-2] in third grade seemed to confirm the substance of these extrapolations."

Here again, my friend's experience with Rosa and my experiences with thousands of children tell us that body language or even one word can and does make an impression on a child whose talk results in positive attention (Greenberg, 1996; Pallak et al., 1982). Furthermore, repeated use of a quick response, such as "Wow!", not only enhances a child's intrinsic motivation to give repeated performances but is also a motivator for children to seek out and then use other big words (Henderlong & Lepper, 2002; Pallak et al., 1982).

History tells us—as do folks on our family trees—that children have always been "quite the talkers." Studies by Cazden (1972), Chomsky (1972), and White (1984) clearly indicate, however, that one's ancestors have had more than a tad to do with all that talking. Indeed, these researchers and others report that what children take in—receptive language—and what they begin to talk—expressive language—are the language and vocabulary they hear being spoken around them. Cullinan (1987, 5)

adds that "the richer the language environment, the richer the language learning."

Later studies by Hart & Risley (1995, 1999) offer insights into the language learning of babies and toddlers, with conclusive evidence that children experience—thus, bring to school with them—vastly different oral language environments with regard to the number and type of words they hear. Such differences can vary, they concluded, by as many as 30 million words by the time children are four years old. In-home records gained in these longitudinal studies not only point to the critical importance of an abundance of language, but also reveal that regardless of such factors as the parent's education attainment, intelligence, socioeconomic level, and race, a child's early and intentional immersion in conversation can reliably predict the child's successes in school-related learning.

Giving Children Words

Ask a kid-enticing question, and one readily witnesses a child's eagerness to join in an oral language dance, to engage in reciprocal conversation, the asking and telling that go back and forth between two or more persons. Kids do like to talk and, generally, they can be readily drawn into conversation. But how much and which vocabulary do they bring to that conversation?

Research and experience tell us that children's oral vocabulary prowess has a direct and positive effect on a student's success as a reader and writer (U.S. Department of Education, 1987). Similarly, Biemiller & Slonim (2001) found that "Because limited vocabulary has been recognized as a key factor in the achievement gap for students with learning disabilities, students of color, and English-language learners, teachers need to seek out and employ vocabulary development activities that provide access to students of all backgrounds and abilities." And Graves (2006) states: "Kindling students' interest and engagement with words is a vital part of helping all students, but especially less advantaged students, to develop rich and powerful vocabularies" (p. 120).

WOW! Words encourages children to bring big words to their conversations. Once children begin to talk, their oral vocabularies increase in direct proportion to the amount of talk in their environments (Hart & Risley, 1995, 1999). Beyond those earliest years, with the exception of occasional oral lessons around content-specific vocabulary, children's instruction on new words involves reading and writing print—regardless of children's abilities to read or write. Unlike oral lessons, printed words lack helpful strategies and clues, such as pronunciation, voice inflections, or body language, important cues that children come to rely on with oral language (Beck, McKeown, Kucan, 2002).

The oral focus of *WOW! Words* not only allows all children to participate, regardless of skill mastery in reading and writing; it invites children to experience one oral success after another. Furthermore, *WOW! Words* provides for children's introduction to vivid figurative expressions. Such oral experiences with figurative language are especially helpful for children who are learning English as a second language (National Institute for Literacy, 2009).

Research, teacher-training, and parent-education programs facilitate intentional or direct instruction of vocabulary. Collins (2005) suggests intentional introduction of "big" words, along with word definitions and synonyms: big words about concepts of literacy, big words that place events in time, and big words about concepts within the various content areas. Further, educators and families are encouraged to extend meaningful talk around big words through use of gestures, sentences, and contextual structures. *WOW! Words* invites children to actively engage in conversations; it provides intentional oral modeling of big words and encourages children to adopt and use those big words.

The long-established work of Vygotsky (1978), which references the "zone of proximal development," heartily supports the notion that, with help, children can reach outside of the norm, the usual, the expected. In summarizing research-based strategies for building children's vocabularies, Pappano (2008) reports that researchers and classroom practitioners agree on the importance of immersing children in language that is considered crucial to success in school—

language found in homes of "privileged" children. Providing more equalized language experiences allows all children access to "high-level talk with rich vocabulary they can absorb and make their own." Also, "building a sophisticated vocabulary at an early age is key to raising reading success—and narrowing the achievement gap" (pp. 1–3).

When considering word selection, educators are encouraged to introduce to children words that work and to rely on "their best judgment, based on an understanding of their students' needs…." They are told that there's "no basis for determining which words students should be learning at different grade levels." Furthermore, in identifying age-appropriateness for a word, the word needs to simply be easy to define and be useful and interesting to children (Beck, McKeown, and Kucan, 2002, 20, 28).

As early as 1925, Whipple noted how words that are in children's speaking vocabularies are less likely to baffle them as readers. More recently, theory and practice in the education of young children underline the importance of oral vocabulary skills as they relate to improvements in literacy rates and, later, in an individual's world of work. Similarly, studies show that children learn vocabulary in the process of daily living, playing, and interacting with others. In line with researchers' encouragement to provide extended instruction that offers active engagement with vocabulary, *WOW! Words* lessons invite children to use and reuse words over time and to interact with the words and their meanings in various contexts (Dyson, 1983; Morrow and Rand, 1991; Teale, 1978).

WOW! Words: Building Children's Powerful Oral Vocabularies (Ages 4–7) provides enticing age-appropriate words and activities such that every young child can, like three-year-old Rosa, grab a listener's attention and engage that listener in meaningful conversation. *WOW! Words* makes it easy to ensure that every child has an ongoing purposeful invitation to join in an oral language dance—interacting orally with others—to gain immersion in rich oral language and in the knowledge embedded within that language. This oral interaction not only helps children develop an impressive speaking and listening vocabulary; it also encourages children to feel confident in using that language in daily conversations with folks of all ages. Those conversational partners listen with interest when a child speaks words and knowledge with confidence. And, like Rosa's aunt, those oral language dance partners invariably exclaim, "Wow!"

Bibliography

Beck, I. L., M. G. McKeown, and L. Kucan. 2002. *Bringing Words to Life: Robust Vocabulary Instruction*. New York: Guilford Press.

Biemiller, A., and N. Slonim. 2001. "Estimating Root Word Vocabulary Growth in Normative and Advantaged Populations: Evidence for a Common Sequence of Vocabulary Acquisition." *Journal of Educational Psychology* 93, no. 3: 498–520.

Cazden, C. 1972. *Child Language and Education*. New York: Holt.

Chomsky, C. 1972. "Stages in Language Development and Reading Exposure." *Harvard Educational Review* 42:1–33.

Collins, M. F. 2005. "ESL Preschoolers' English Vocabulary Acquisition from Storybook Reading." *Reading Research Quarterly* 40, no. 4:406–408.

Cullinan, B. E., ed. 1987. *Children's Literature in the Reading Program*. Newark, DE: International Reading Association.

Dyson, A. H. 1983. "The Role of Oral Language in Early Writing Processes." *Research in the Teaching of English* 17, no. 1:1–25.

Graves, M. F. 2006. *The Vocabulary Book: Learning & Instruction*. New York: Teachers College Press.

Greenberg, P. 1996. "How and When to Praise." *Parent & Child*. http://www2.scholastic.com/browse/article.jsp?id=2064.

Hart, B., and T. R. Risley. 1995. *Meaningful Differences in the Everyday Experience of Young American Children*. Baltimore: Brookes Publishing.

———. 1999. *Learning to Talk: The Social World of Children*. Baltimore: Brookes Publishing.

Henderlong, J., and M. R. Lepper. 2002. "The Effects of Praise on Children's Intrinsic Motivation: A Review and Synthesis," *Psychological Bulletin* 128, no. 5:774–795.

Morrow, L. M., and M. K. Rand. 1991. "Promoting Literacy During Play by Designing Early Childhood Classroom Environments." *Reading Teacher* 44, no. 6:396–402.

National Institute for Literacy. 2009. "About the Partnership for Reading." Washington, DC: National Institute for Literacy. http://www.nifl.gov/partnershipforreading/publications/reading_first1vocab.html.

Pallak, S. R., S. Costomiris, S. Sroka, and T. S. Pittman. 1982. "School Experience, Reward Characteristics, and Intrinsic Motivation." *Child Development* 53:1382–1391.

Pappano, L. 2008. "Small Kids, Big Words: Research-based Strategies for Building Vocabulary from PreK to Grade 3." *Harvard Education Letter* 24:1–3.

Roskos, K. A., P. O. Tabors, and L. A. Lenhart. 2009. *Oral Language and Early Literacy in Preschool: Talking, Reading, and Writing*, 2nd ed. Newark, DE: International Reading Association.

Teale, W. H. 1978. "Positive Environments for Learning to Read: What Studies of Early Readers Tell Us." *Language Arts* 55, no. 8: 922–932.

U.S. Department of Education. 1987. *What Works: Research about Teaching and Learning*. Washington, DC: U.S. Department of Education.

Vygotsky, L. 1987. "Interaction Between Learning and Development." In *Mind in Society*, trans. M. Cole, 79–91 Cambridge, MA: Harvard University Press.

Whipple, G. M., ed. 1925. *The Twenty-fourth Yearbook of the National Society for the Study of Education: Report of the National Committee on Reading*. Bloomington, IL: Public School Publishing Company.

White, D. 1984. *Books Before Five*. Portsmouth, NH: Heinemann.

How to Use This Book

This collection contains 144 WOW! Word lessons, which are intended to enrich the listening and speaking vocabularies of young children ages 4 through 7. The lessons appear in four groups of 36 lessons each, allowing for one new word each week for each age group—4s, 5s, 6s, and 7s—throughout a school year. Each lesson focuses on the oral introduction of one WOW! Word or *Word Of the Week.*

In a WOW! Word's lesson, you'll find a variety of suggested ways to model the word's use orally all week long as children go about everyday activities in the classroom or at home. Many teachers and parents report how they practice a casual introduction of a week's new WOW! Word each Monday by simply speaking the word or one of its forms within the context of their morning greeting or while going about any routine activity or discussion. Using the word orally as often as three times each day during the week helps children gain confidence in using the word in their own speech. Ideally, each successive week's WOW! Word joins continued and ongoing use of previous weeks' words such that children's vocabularies increase gradually and consistently.

Each lesson's comprehensive ideas and suggestions provide various ways to incorporate the WOW! Word throughout the year. This ongoing modeling allows you to add to children's listening and speaking vocabularies a minimum of 36 meaningful and useful big words during the year. The lessons present ways to stimulate children's awareness of comparable big words they hear others speak, words they, too, could use in conversations.

Additionally, you will find that the many practical and comprehensive ideas and suggestions aid you in using the words and lessons in differentiated instruction that best meets the needs of your children, individually and collectively. Numerous activities involve children's use of

pictures and photographs that are readily available in old magazines and newspapers. The visual emphasis helps very young children and special-needs students associate oral language—words and sentences they hear and speak—with knowledge embedded in that language. Additionally, pictures help children call on their life experiences and use imagination to organize and express thoughts and ideas orally to tell stories about what they think is happening in a picture or photograph. Children also gain practice in the use of oral language and mastery of grammar skills in word forms and verb tenses as they talk about what they think may have happened before or after a pictured event.

This book is designed so that the WOW! Words lessons may be presented corresponding to children's ages or in another sequence that suits your individual needs. To assist you in locating particular words, the WOW! Words lessons are arranged in alphabetical order within the four age groups. Look for the following categories (included as appropriate to each WOW! Word) to help you present each word orally to your young listeners and speakers:

Pronunciation
Here's What It Means
Synonyms
Figuratively Speaking
Forms of the Word to Share
Talk & Share
Focusing Talk™
Hands-on Activity
WOW! Rhyme™

In this book's back matter you will find tools to assist you in organizing and/or displaying the WOW! Words as you present them. You will find patterns to duplicate and cut out to create and display any one of four WOW! Words characters. Adding a segment or link to a character each week not only supports and encourages children's

---

Focusing Talk is a trademark of Babs Bell Hajdusiewicz. WOW! Rhyme is a trademark of Babs Bell Hajdusiewicz.

interest in using WOW! Words; it can also help your organization of words as you introduce them. In addition, a displayed character may well offer you a visual prompt to use the words in your daily conversations and interactions with children.

You may also want to maintain a collection of pictures to help children visualize and integrate a WOW! Word in daily conversations and interactions. For example, a picture of a person who's eager to open a package can help to illustrate *anticipate* (5s); a picture of someone looking through a window helps illustrate *transparent* (7s).

The WOW! Words lessons are intended for use in enriching children's *listening* and *speaking* vocabularies. You will, therefore, want to focus on the oral language aspects of listening and speaking to avoid any expectation for children to read or write the big words, or WOW! Words. In the event that a child announces an ability to read or write a WOW! Word, you may want to respond, "Wow!" and move on. While such a response recognizes the child's excitement in having gained a new skill, it also maintains the integrity and age-appropriateness of this oral-only program. The letter to family members reinforces this focus on successes with oral vocabulary. Similarly, a lesson's mention of reading or writing is intended to point out opportunities for you to model for children how talk can be written and how print can be spoken.

Pronunciation

Following are some guidelines for your reference and ease in pronouncing each WOW! Word. Like most of us, children are apt to repeat a word exactly the way they first hear it. This is especially true when ears hear a word for the first time.

You'll find the guidelines for pronunciation especially helpful as you prepare to first introduce a WOW! Word. As in most dictionaries, the guidelines focus on the *sounds* one actually hears in a word. For example, the letter *k* represents the sound of *c* as heard in *cat*. Because these pronunciation guidelines are for your eyes only, for the purposes of this resource book, capital letters

are used to indicate a word's accented syllable, the part of a word you will emphasize orally, much like you might use the tone of your voice to help a listener pay particular attention to a word or name as you talk. And for your added ease, you will note an absence of special marks, such as accent and diacritical marks. You may, of course, consult a dictionary should you have any question about a word's pronunciation.

The following pronunciation guide will help you prepare to introduce each WOW! Word exactly as it sounds:

1. Schwa sound is spelled *uh: come = kuhm*

2. Long vowel sound is spelled as double letter *aa, ee, ii, oo, uu*. EXCEPTION: *oo* heard in *tooth* spelled *uu* for *tuuth*

3. Short vowel sound is spelled as single letter *a, e, i, o, u: a* heard in *bath; e* heard in *bed; i* heard in *ink; o* heard in *mom; u* heard in *nut*

4. Vowel sound heard in *ball, shawl, bought* spelled *aw* for *bawl, shawl, bawt*

5. Y's sound in *very* is spelled *ee = VAIR ee*

6. Y's sound in *why* is spelled *ii = whii*

7. R-controlled vowel sound is spelled *ur* as in *perk = purk, dirt = durt*. EXCEPTIONS: *pork = pork; park = park*

8. R-controlled vowel digraph sound of *air* is spelled *air* as in *airfare = AIR fair; clarify = KLAIR uh fii*

9. R-controlled vowel digraph sound of *ear* is spelled *eer: tier = teer; weird = weerd; cheer = cheer*

10. R-controlled vowel digraph sound of *ow* is spelled *ow: proud = prowd; hour = owr*

11. Diphthong sound of *aw* is spelled *aw: haul = hawl; crawl = krawl; awkward = AWK wurd*

12. Diphthong sound of *oi* is spelled *oy: boy = boy; noisy = NOY zee*

13. Schwa sound followed by *l* is spelled *uhl: able = AA buhl*

14. Sound of *x* blended with other letters, such as heard in *exaggerate* or *exceedingly,* is spelled *g*

followed by *z*: *ig ZA juh raat* or *k* followed by *s* = *ek SEE ding lee*

15. Sound of *u* heard in *view* = *yuu*
16. Sound of *qu* heard in *quick* = *kw*

Here's What It Means

Here you will find a helpful definition for the WOW! Word, along with its part of speech when used in context. Occasionally, you'll find a word can be used meaningfully in more than one way. In this case, additional uses are listed, along with corresponding part(s) of speech.

Synonyms

This section provides a list of selected synonyms and word phrases that have nearly the same meaning as the WOW! Word. During conversations, you will want to use these words and phrases interchangeably with the *Word Of the Week*. Such use not only helps children gain meaning from a new word; it also models the use of synonyms. In addition, your modeling of synonyms emphasizes the purpose and value of a reference book or online resource, such as a dictionary or thesaurus. While you'll find a long list of synonyms for some WOW! Words, other lists will be short. The lists will help you keep all synonyms meaningful, useful, and age-appropriate. As you and children interact using a WOW! Word, you will want to note in the margins of the lesson any additional synonyms or phrases that are especially meaningful and useful for children.

Figuratively Speaking

In some lessons, you'll find, as applicable, one or more figures of speech that will provide you with yet another way to use a WOW! Word's meaning in conversation with children. Figurative language is particularly helpful for children who are learning English as a second language. You will want to be mindful of how some figures of speech are common to a particular community or region of the country and how talkers and writers often coin new figures of speech—such as "Google it" to indicate a need to search the Internet to find

information on a topic. Thus, as you and children interact using a WOW! Word, you will want to note in the margins of a lesson any additional idioms or clichés that are especially meaningful and useful for children.

Forms of the Word to Share

Here you will find selected forms of a WOW! Word to assist you as you model use of the word in context. Each word form is listed with its part of speech when used in context. For some words, you'll find no list of forms. This is in keeping with this book's goal of presenting words that are meaningful and useful to the targeted age child. Occasionally, you'll find a word form can be used meaningfully in more than one way. In this case, each additional use is listed, along with its corresponding part(s) of speech. As with lists of synonyms and figurative language, you will find here word forms that children will find useful and meaningful in their daily conversations and interactions. Similarly, you will want to note in the margins of a lesson any additional forms your children suggest.

Another Meaning

A handful of lessons contain this section to help you sort out these words that have more than one meaning. You'll find the word's meaning, along with its classified part of speech when used in context. Experiences with multiple-meaning words are especially helpful for children who are learning English as a second language.

Talk & Share

Look here for examples of age-appropriate, meaningful, conversational sentences, each of which includes the WOW! Word or a form of the word. Ten sentences are provided as suggestions to help get you started in modeling the use of the word and its forms during everyday conversations throughout a year. Frequent modeling of the week's WOW! Word helps children add the word to their personal vocabularies for use at home or wherever they find opportunities for conversation. For example, modeling of a sentence, such as

"Albert Einstein had an analytical mind" (WOW! Word: *analyze*, 5s), sparked a kindergarten girl's astute observation: "Jason has an analytical mind!" In addition, the sentences will stimulate you and your children to create new and different sentences, oral ideas you will want to write in the page margins for later reference in reinforcing a word's concept.

Focusing Talk™

This section offers practical and easy suggestions for modeling the use of the WOW! Word during your daily conversations with children. Some of the suggestions focus on ways to present WOW! Word–related figurative language. Such experiences are especially helpful for children who are learning English as a second language. Other suggestions provide meaningful ways to converse with children using various forms of a WOW! Word. As you and the children "live" with a WOW! Word, its forms, and its meanings, you'll want to jot in the margins your own ideas for Focusing Talk around the word. Many activities reference poems and songs that you will find listed in the Resources section at the back of this book. While you will find entire texts for many of the referenced materials, the resource lists will help you locate other recommended poems, books, or folklore.

Hands-on Activity

Look here for a WOW! Word-related activity that involves children in the practical use of the word, its forms, and the meaning of each form. You will notice some suggestions recommend the use of old magazines and newspapers. The ready access to such visual aids not only stimulates children's awareness of print in their surroundings; such visual aids also help children associate pictured ideas with meaningful oral language they have heard and spoken. Numerous activity ideas will not only assist your planning to meet all your children's needs in a multi-age setting; the activities are also well-suited for use in daily routines and in your learning centers. Again, some activities reference poems and songs that you will find listed in the Resources section at the back of this book. While you will find entire texts for many of the referenced materials, resource lists will help you locate other recommended poems, books, or folklore.

WOW! Rhyme™

This final section of each lesson features a fun rhyme that focuses on the WOW! Word and/ or one or more of its forms. You will find the WOW! Word's meaning tucked into the context of each WOW! Rhyme. While some rhymes offer suggestions for singing to a familiar tune, you'll find that each rhyme's language and meter invite you and the children to say the rhyme as a chant or to singsong it. (To singsong a rhyme, merely add a springy dancing feel to your voice. And some rhymes, such as WOW! Rhyme: *discourage*, 5s, nearly dance on their own!) WOW! Rhymes make frequent use of humor and surprise, because these elements, along with rhythm and rhyme, invite children to want to hear a rhyme again to learn and then repeat its words. Indeed, repetition helps us all retain language we hear.

You may want to read, chant, singsong, or sing the WOW! Rhyme several times when you first introduce a WOW! Word. As you repeat the rhyme each day, invite children to join in to say it with you chorally. You'll find other creative ways to utilize the WOW! Rhyme, such as to recite the rhyme during wait times or while transitioning from one activity to another. With repetition, children might choose to say the rhyme individually or chorally as you "take dictation" on chart paper, thereby modeling the writing of children's spoken words on paper. Although there is no focus on children's reading or writing the WOW! Words and WOW! Rhymes, your recording rhymes children have learned to say through repetition presents a valuable and not-to-be-missed opportunity—to model the very essence of reading and writing. This scribing of children's talk is an excellent way to help children recognize that all print they see—in books, newspapers, magazines, computer screens, signage, and so on—is simply talk that's "written down." Occasionally, as in the WOW! Words lesson for *threaten* (5s), a WOW! Rhyme not only helps children use the WOW! Word but also presents another big word in meaningful context.

Blackline Masters

Use the blackline masters beginning on page 164 of this book to help you record the introduction and ongoing use of each WOW! Word. The patterns are designed to help you create any one of four unique displays. With the addition of a new WOW! Word each week, your display might seem to grow during the year, as do children's listening and speaking vocabularies.

Patterns are included to help you create: a train that may add a boxcar each week, a caterpillar that adds a segment, a family of ducks that adds a duckling, or a fish in a fishbowl that adds a bubble.

To create your display of choice, reproduce its first pattern, cut out the shape, and use markers or buttons, beads, craft items, and the like, to add facial features. Each successive week, reproduce the chosen design's corresponding pattern, cut out its shape, and attach it in place to indicate the "new-word growth." You may wish to write the new *Word Of the Week* on the added segment. Children may choose to mark dots or apply sticky

dots, stars, or the like to a segment to indicate each use of the WOW! Word they've heard themselves or others speak. Children might also indicate uses of a word vertically by attaching sticky notes to simulate a tail or added "appendage" that hangs down from the appropriate segment.

Creating a WOW! Words display promotes continued use of all familiar WOW! Words. Alternatively, you might record the introduction of WOW! Words on a classroom calendar.

In this section, you will also find a reproducible take-home letter for your ease in sharing WOW! Words with family members. You can copy and send home this letter as you introduce each new *WOW! Words* lesson.

Indexes

Various indexes at the back of the book help you locate specific information contained in this book. You will find all WOW! Words and their lessons indexed alphabetically, by suggested age group, and by theme and skill. You will also find an index of those recommended poems and songs for which complete texts are included. In addition, an Index by First Lines helps you locate WOW! Rhymes and their related WOW! Words. Additional poems and songs are similarly indexed.

AGE 4

- ☐ absolutely
- ☐ accurate
- ☐ annoy
- ☐ complicated
- ☐ consider
- ☐ contribute
- ☐ curious
- ☐ determined
- ☐ disgusting
- ☐ exaggerate
- ☐ examine
- ☐ exhausted
- ☐ expand
- ☐ fascinating
- ☐ fragile
- ☐ immediately
- ☐ inquire
- ☐ interrupt

- ☐ mammoth
- ☐ maximum
- ☐ minimum
- ☐ mysterious
- ☐ numerous
- ☐ opinion
- ☐ participate
- ☐ positive
- ☐ predicament
- ☐ predict
- ☐ propose
- ☐ recognize
- ☐ ridiculous
- ☐ suspicious
- ☐ thoughtful
- ☐ urgent
- ☐ valuable
- ☐ vehicle

Here's What It Means

adverb: for sure

Synonyms—*They have nearly the same meaning.*

completely   really
definitely   without a doubt
positively

Figuratively Speaking

yep; yup; yes; you bet; it's so

Form of *absolutely* to Share with 4s

absolute (adjective)

Talk & Share

1. I absolutely cannot see from here.

2. I'm going to sit in absolute quiet.

3. Do you think that's absolutely true?

4. There are absolutely no crayons left in the box.

5. It absolutely cannot rain today!

6. I absolutely love snow!

7. What I told you was the absolute truth.

8. Yes, it's absolutely time to clean up.

9. I have absolutely no reason to believe that.

10. We need to feel absolutely safe.

Focusing Talk: Finding Absolute Truths

Help children classify statements as "absolutely true" or "absolutely not true." Model examples, as appropriate, such as "It's hot outside today. That's absolutely true!" or "It's cold outside today. That's absolutely not true!" With practice, have children initiate statements for others to classify as absolutely true or absolutely not true. Encourage interchangeable use of the words *false* and *not true*.

Hands-On: Making Absolute Shape Identifications

Provide paper circles and squares of differing sizes for children to sort into a group of circles and a group of squares. Model describing a shape as follows: "This shape is absolutely round," or "This shape is absolutely square." Have children follow your model to describe shapes as they use clothes hangers, string, and the paper shapes to create interesting mobiles. At other times, repeat the activity to include rectangles or triangles.

WOW! Rhyme: ***absolutely***

It's absolutely true.

It is!

That's why I'm telling you.

It happened to me.

It did.

It did.

It's absolutely true!

accurate (AK yur uht)

Here's What It Means

adjective: right; correct

Synonyms—*They have nearly the same meaning.*

correct   to the point
exact   without mistakes
okay

Figuratively Speaking

right on

Forms of *accurate* to Share with 4s

accuracy (noun)
accurately (adverb)
inaccurate (adjective)
inaccurately (adverb)

Talk & Share

1. Dad likes his watch to be accurate.
2. Your answers have been accurate so far.
3. I know I am accurate about this.
4. I don't think your math is accurate here.
5. Do you think the price is inaccurate?
6. His story can't be accurate.
7. I see the weather report was accurate.
8. Accuracy is important when paying for something.
9. I think you repeated that accurately.
10. My name is spelled inaccurately on that list.

Focusing Talk: Seeking Accuracy

Model how one might check for accuracy what another person says. For example, say, "A pencil can break," and help a partner say, "That is accurate." Then say, "Dogs have wings," and help the partner reply, "That is inaccurate." Invite partners to take turns following the model to check for accuracy as they converse. Remind children that to be polite sometimes means we might think something but choose not to say it.

Hands-On: Matching for Accuracy

Provide drawing paper and five different-sized circular objects, such as buttons, blocks, a cup's rim, lids, or a cookie cutter. Have each child draw around the five objects to have five circles on one sheet of paper. Then shuffle the children's papers, give one to each child, and invite children to accurately match each circle to the object used to draw it. Encourage use of *accurate* and *accuracy* as matches are made.

WOW! Rhyme: **accurate**

I try to be accurate.
I like to be right.
But if I am wrong,
I'll still be polite.

Here's What It Means

verb: to bother

Synonyms—*They have nearly the same meaning.*

disturb
irritate
upset

Figuratively Speaking

bug; drive up the wall; drive nuts

Forms of *annoy* to Share with 4s

annoyance (noun)
annoyed (verb, adjective)
annoying (verb, adjective)
annoys (verb)

Talk & Share

1. It annoys me when I can't do something.
2. A barking dog can annoy people.
3. It annoyed me when my pencil broke in half.
4. This broken zipper is an annoyance.
5. My grandma seemed annoyed when she talked to me.
6. Sometimes your behavior annoys me.
7. Your behavior does not annoy me now.
8. Nothing has annoyed me today.
9. How might we fix an annoying leak?
10. The noise outside is annoying me.

Focusing Talk: Identifying Annoying and Pleasing Things

Ask why this sentence doesn't make sense: "A broken zipper *pleases* me." Help children notice that it would make sense to change the word *pleases* to *annoys*. Discuss how the words *annoys* and *pleases* are opposite in meaning. Help children use *annoys* or *pleases* in complete sentences to tell about personal experiences when things have annoyed or pleased them. Encourage children to tell why they have been annoyed or pleased.

Hands-On: Dramatizing Annoyances

Invite partners to be gentle and kind to each other as they take turns to act out annoying behaviors, such as repeatedly tapping fingers or feet to make noise or interrupting when the partner is talking. Have children come to a community circle to share their experiences about which behaviors were, indeed, annoyances. Encourage children to tell family members about this activity and tell what they learned about behaviors that annoy others.

WOW! Rhyme: *annoy*

When my friend doesn't share,
It's annoying.
When a sock or shoe hides,
It's annoying.
When I can't go to sleep,
It's annoying.
Oops! Are all my annoyances...
annoying?

complicated (KOM pli kaa tid)

Here's What It Means

adjective: very difficult

verb: to have made something very difficult

Synonyms—*They have nearly the same meaning.*

challenging	hard to do
confusing	puzzling

Forms of *complicated* to Share with 4s

complicate (verb)

complicates (verb)

complicating (verb)

complication (noun)

Talk & Share

1. This is much too complicated to do right now.

2. His busy schedule is complicating our dinner hour.

3. There are complications that make the job impossible.

4. I'm sorry the directions to my house are so complicated.

5. It complicated my day when I couldn't find my shoe.

6. Braids are complicated, so it took a long time to get ready.

7. Ironing a shirt looks complicated.

8. Mom says a new cell phone could complicate her life.

9. The directions for making breakfast are complicated!

10. It complicates my life when my hair gets tangled.

Focusing Talk:
Discussing Complicated Situations

Tell about a complicated situation you've encountered. An example might be a stack or row of books that keeps falling down. Talk about the cause for the complication (too many books) and a possible resolution (remove some books; get help). Help children share complicated situations they've faced, the causes, and possible resolutions. Children will enjoy your use of the words *resolution* and *resolve* as they share experiences.

Hands-On:
Tangling and Untangling

Display a chenille stick that's tied in a loose knot. Talk about how easy, or not very complicated, it can be to untangle a loose knot as you straighten the stick. Now form two loops and demonstrate untangling them as you talk about how this untangling task seems a bit more complicated. Help partners use forms of *complicate* to talk as they work to tie and untie knots. Avoiding tight knots, invite pairs to present complicated knots to others.

WOW! Rhyme: **complicated**

It was difficult.

So complicated.

It wasn't easy to do.

But I tried it again,

and again,

and look!

I've figured it out for you!

Here's What It Means
verb: to think about

Synonyms—*They have nearly the same meaning.*
care about
think about
ponder (See WOW! Word: *ponder,* page 117.)

Figuratively Speaking
mull over

Forms of *consider* to Share with 4s
considerate (adjective)
consideration (noun)
considered (verb)
considering (verb)
considers (verb)
inconsiderate (adjective)

Talk & Share
1. We need to consider everyone's opinions.
2. Every day, she considers sharing her lunch with her friend.
3. It's considerate to thank someone for a gift.
4. I didn't consider that the toys belonged to you.
5. Grabbing things is really inconsiderate.
6. Thank you for considering my needs.
7. I am considering going to sleep now.
8. We have time for more consideration if you like.
9. I'm considering what you said.
10. It takes time to consider all these choices.

Focusing Talk: Considering Interests and Behaviors
Tell children that you consider it fun to read or ski or do another activity you enjoy. Invite children to follow your model to tell about things they consider to be fun. Repeat for activities you consider boring or dangerous or exhausting. Help children use consider and its forms in each example. At another time, help children name behaviors that are considered to be considerate versus behaviors that are deemed inconsiderate.

Hands-On: Considering Original Ideas
Help each child free-draw two circles side by side to represent two suns, or add stems and consider the circles to represent two apples or two oranges. Now ask children to color one of their objects its usual color and the other object a different color. Model how children might tell about their objects in sentences, such as: *The moon is yellow, but consider this… I made a purple moon!*

WOW! Rhyme: *consider*
Consider how terribly kind I am.
Consider how often I share.
Consider that I am your very best friend.
Hey… may I have that toy over there?

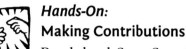

Here's What It Means

verb: to give

Synonyms—*They have nearly the same meaning.*

donate   pitch in
furnish   provide
participate   supply

Forms of *contribute* to Share with 4s

contributed (verb)
contributes (verb)
contributing (verb)
contribution (noun)
contributor (noun)

Talk & Share

1. I want to contribute to help us win.

2. My contribution is ready.

3. I am the contributor of most of this stuff.

4. My mom contributed cookies for the bake sale.

5. This big contribution is wonderful.

6. I'm happy to see you contribute your ideas.

7. Aunt Martha contributes to her favorite charity every year.

8. My dad said he contributed for himself and me.

9. I will think of a way I can contribute.

10. How are you contributing to this project?

 Contributing to a Conversation

Introduce a topic by using a complete sentence, such as *I like cats*. Invite a child to follow your complete-sentence model to add to or contribute to the conversation such that sentences relate to one another. For example, a contributor might add, "I like cats, too." Encourage others to contribute to the conversation until it appears to be time to begin a new topic sentence. This activity helps children relate to one another and to stay on topic.

 *Hands-On:*
Making Contributions

Read aloud *Stone Soup* (see Resources, page 173). Talk about the ingredients that were contributed to make the soup in this story. Then invite partners or small groups to cut out pictures of foods they might contribute to make a pot of soup. Encourage children to tell about each contribution in a complete sentence, such as *I am contributing [named item]*, or *My contribution is [named item]*.

WOW! Rhyme: **contribute**

(*Note:* Children may sing this rhyme to the tune of "The Farmer in the Dell.")

At contribution time,
At contribution time,
I like to give what I can give
at contribution time.

Here's What It Means

adjective: want to know about

Synonyms—*They have nearly the same meaning.*

eager to learn	interested
nosy	tuned in
wonder about	looking for information

Figuratively Speaking

like George; like a cat

Forms of *curious* to Share with 4s

curiosity (noun)
curiously (adverb)

Talk & Share

1. I am curious when I hear an unfamiliar noise.

2. I am curious about growing up and going to college.

3. I'm curious, but I have to go now.

4. Mom said her curiosity caused her to ask more questions.

5. I'm curious to see if you will like that book.

6. Cats act so curiously when they inspect everything.

7. Curious George asked lots of questions.

8. My curiosity helped me find a leaky pipe under the sink.

9. Sometimes I'm curious, but this book doesn't interest me.

10. She was curious to see how high he could stack the blocks.

Focusing Talk: Sharing Curiosities

Read aloud a *Curious George* book (see Resources, page 173). Discuss George's curiosities and a reason for each. Model sharing an interest of yours by saying, "I am curious about (topic). I am curious about (topic) because…." Help children follow your model to share their curiosities. Remind partners to take turns so that one listens as the other talks. Monitor conversations to help children include a reason that prompts each curiosity.

Hands-On: Discussing Curious Details

Invite partners to identify pictures in magazines or newspapers that cause them to feel some amount of curiosity. Examples might include: a wrapped gift, a face that shows strong emotion, an accident scene, an empty refrigerator, someone talking animatedly on a phone, an emergency vehicle, or an animal running. Help partners describe details in the pictures that prompted curiosity and what they think may have happened to cause those details.

WOW! Rhyme: **curious**

Everyone called me Curious George,
and I know why they did.
I asked a lot of questions, because
I am a curious kid.

Here's What It Means

adjective: feeling sure of
verb: decided

Synonyms—*They have nearly the same meaning.*

definite about   settled on
firm   stubborn
intent

Figuratively Speaking

showing some muscle; hanging in there; driven

Forms of *determined* to Share with 4s

determine (verb)
determines (verb)
determining (verb)
determination (noun)

Talk & Share

1. We were determined to play after school.

2. The weather may determine what we will do.

3. My brother's homework sometimes determines his bedtime.

4. I get to determine how I'd like to celebrate.

5. I am determined to find a solution.

6. Who is determining the rules for this game?

7. The little engine was determined to chug up the hill.

8. She is determined to make everyone follow the rules.

9. I was determined to finish the book before I went to bed.

10. Dad noticed my determination to climb the rock wall.

Focusing Talk: Feeling Determined

Encourage children to think about how they feel when they want very much to do something, such as learn to tie a shoe, hit a ball, ride a bicycle, or cut with scissors. Invite children to tell about times when they or a friend or family member have seemed determined to do something. Ask why they think the person was determined. Ask whether determination helped the person. Allow for varying opinions.

Hands-On: Determining Matches

Provide squares, rectangles, triangles, and circles, all in various sizes. Invite children to determine which objects have the same shape and group them accordingly. Then have partners determine size gradations to arrange each group of shapes from smallest to largest. At another time, as appropriate, provide two sets of numbers from 0 to 9, alphabet letters, colored pieces of paper, or pictures for children to determine matches.

WOW! Rhyme: **determined**

I'm determined to be
the best I can be.
Determined I am!
I'll be my best ME!

Here's What It Means

adjective: very upsetting

Synonyms—*They have nearly the same meaning.*

distasteful　　　very annoying
offensive　　　　very disagreeable

Forms of *disgusting* to Share with 4s

disgust (verb)
disgusted (verb, adjective)
disgusts (verb)

Talk & Share

1. What behavior might disgust your mom?

2. I thought his behavior was disgusting.

3. Aunt Billee says that the dog hair on the couch is disgusting.

4. Is there a food that has a disgusting taste?

5. Dad says some music is disgusting.

6. I felt disgusted when no one came to support the fundraiser.

7. My messy face disgusted me!

8. It disgusts my grandma when someone shows bad manners.

9. It's disgusting to mistreat an animal.

10. I think it's disgusting to be mean to someone.

Focusing Talk:
Identifying Disgusting Things

Read "It's a Fact!" (see Resources, page 178). Then write "Disgusting Things" on chart paper and invite children to name things they think are disgusting. List all ideas, allowing for differing opinions and defense of ideas as children talk about why an idea seems disgusting to them. Encourage children to use *disgusting* or its forms in sentences, such as "I think being selfish is disgusting" or "It's disgusting to talk while chewing food."

Hands-On:
Making a Book of Disgusting Things

Share poems, such as "Goops" by Gelett Burgess (see Resources, page 174) or "Disorder." Invite children to think about the poems along with their own ideas as they search old magazines to cut out pictures that show disgusting things. Help children dictate the use of *disgusting* in sentences to tell about each picture. Help children create a book titled "Disgusting Things" and then take turns sharing the class book at home with family members.

WOW! Rhyme: **disgusting**

It's disgusting.
I don't like it.
It's offensive to my nose.
It's disgusting
and it's stinkier
than sweaty, stinky toes.

Here's What It Means

verb: to stretch the truth

Synonyms—*They have nearly the same meaning.*

boast

brag

make greater

Figuratively Speaking

tell a fish story

Forms of *exaggerate* to Share with 4s

exaggerated (verb)

exaggerates (verb)

exaggerating (verb)

exaggeration (noun)

exaggerator (noun)

Talk & Share

1. Mom knew I had not exaggerated.

2. Sometimes I exaggerate a bit.

3. That story was a huge exaggeration.

4. My cousin is sometimes an exaggerator.

5. I didn't exaggerate. I really can swim.

6. Were you exaggerating about being so scared?

7. Does your friend ever exaggerate?

8. I guess I exaggerated about how late I stayed up.

9. Watch out for exaggerations!

10. I know he sometimes exaggerates.

Focusing Talk: Discussing Exaggerations

Read aloud a tall-tale poem, such as "True Story," "Boa Constrictor," "Hungry Mungry" (see Resources, page 174), or "My True Story" (page 179). Help children identify examples of exaggeration in a poem and use a complete sentence, such as *I think it's an exaggeration to say a snake could eat me,* to tell why each example seems to be an exaggeration. Encourage discussion about why each poet might have used exaggeration to tell the story.

Hands-On: Exaggerating with Rubber Bands

Provide rubber bands in various colors, along with varying sizes of cardboard tubes from paper towels, toilet tissue, and gift wrap. Invite children to exaggerate or stretch the rubber bands to connect and/or decorate the tubes. At another time, provide cut rubber bands for children to exaggerate or stretch slowly in proportion to their talking as they share a tall-tale sentence, such as *I played with a real dinosaur and a real giraffe and....*

WOW! Rhyme: **exaggerate**

You know how I exaggerate?

Well, I'll tell you what I just ate.

I ate a boat; I ate its sail.

I ate the sea; I ate a whale.

I warned you I exaggerate.

Do you believe what I just ate?

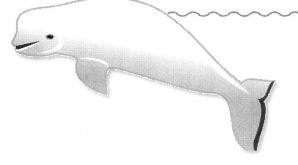

Here's What It Means

verb: to look over carefully

Synonyms—*They have nearly the same meaning.*

consider take a look at
explore test
inspect think about
question

Figuratively Speaking

grill; give the third degree; leave no stone unturned

Forms of *examine* to Share with 4s

examination (noun)
examined (verb)
examining (verb, adjective)

Talk & Share

1. We examined the backpack and found a hole in it.

2. I must wear the cast until the doctor examines my leg again.

3. I had an eye examination today.

4. Uh-oh, my dog is examining my lunch!

5. You can examine it to see if I wrote what you said.

6. After careful examination, we made a new rule.

7. I examined the page to find the information I needed.

8. My sister scored well on her examinations.

9. Could you examine these to be sure they're clean?

10. Dad examined the car for scratches.

Focusing Talk: Examining for Needs

Say, "I examined the weather to determine whether I should bring an umbrella today." Then help children say sentences about examining facts before making decisions. Sentences may include: "I examine my hands to decide if I have dried them," "I examine my hair to check how well I have brushed it," "I examine my shirts and pants to choose colors that go together," or "I examine my pencil to tell if it needs to be sharpened."

Hands-On: Examining to Sort

Provide scraps of various fabrics, such as cotton, lace, corduroy, velvet, wool, denim, rayon, polyester, silk, linen. Invite children to place each fabric type before a window or other light source. Help children examine the swatches and sort them into two groups—those that are transparent (offers the ability to see through) and those that are opaque (do not allow light to pass through). Encourage use of *transparent* and *opaque* in other ways.

WOW! Rhyme: **examine**

They examined this.
They examined that.
The veterinarian examined my cat.
The examination is done, but now
My cat is examining my back—
ME-OW!

exhausted (ig ZAW stid)

Here's What It Means

adjective: very tired; used up

verb: tired; used up

Synonyms—*They have nearly the same meaning.*

drained   without energy

half asleep   worn out

spent

Figuratively Speaking

plumb tuckered out; wiped out; run out of steam

Forms of *exhausted* to Share with 4s

exhaust (verb)

exhausting (verb, adjective)

exhausts (verb)

Talk & Share

1. We were exhausted when we got home.

2. Did you exhaust your supply of paper?

3. Have we exhausted all of the possibilities yet?

4. My grandpa said he felt exhausted after dinner.

5. It was exhausting work to rake leaves all morning.

6. We can keep playing if no one feels exhausted.

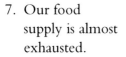

7. Our food supply is almost exhausted.

8. I'm not exhausted yet.

9. Jumping rope sometimes exhausts my great-grandma.

10. Our long conversation is exhausting the battery in my phone.

Focusing Talk: Feeling Exhausted

Dramatize an activity, such as hopping, reading, or cooking, for children to name. Then say, as appropriate, "I sometimes feel exhausted after running." or "I am usually not exhausted after sweeping." Invite children to use forms of *exhaust* to dramatize and name various activities. At another time, invite children to talk in sentences about an activity, such as bike riding, that can be exhausting… until children have exhausted all their ideas.

Hands-On: Identifying Exhausted Things

Provide old magazines for children to identify pictures of items, such as pencils, books, clothes, crayons, or toys that appear to be exhausted or worn out or used up. Have children glue pictures to create book pages for a class book. Write as children tell sentences about how each pictured object may have come to appear exhausted. At another time, create a book that depicts people doing exhausting activities.

WOW! Rhyme: **exhausted**

I was tired and worn out.

Too exhausted to eat.

But I wasn't exhausted

when mom served a treat.

Here's What It Means

verb: to make larger

Synonyms—*They have nearly the same meaning.*

increase   spread out
lengthen   widen

Forms of *expand* to Share with 4s

expandable (adjective)
expanded (verb)
expanding (verb)
expands (verb)

Talk & Share

1. We need to expand our circle.

2. A rubber band expands to hold the sticks together.

3. I am expanding my balloon.

4. My balloon expanded until it popped.

5. Our neighbors expanded their house when the twins were born.

6. I expanded the folder and put in more paper.

7. Grandma says she likes expandable belts.

8. Mom's boss expanded her hours at work so she could earn more money.

9. We need to expand the table so everyone has space.

10. My aunt wants to expand her paycheck.

Focusing Talk: Expanding Ideas

Introduce children to the classic "fish story" by holding out your hands in front of you and slowly increasing the space between them as you show and tell about a fish you caught. Help children understand the humor of expanding the fish's length. Children might tell "fish stories" about a monster in a dream or about how far someone jumped.

Hands-On: Expanding Hand Muscles

Have children hold a rubber band in one hand and stretch the fingers to expand the band. Tell children that this exercises the hand muscles. Encourage children to explore ways to make various shapes and images as they expand a rubber band with one hand, two hands, or two fingers.

WOW! Rhyme: *expand*

I hold it in my fingers
and
I make a rubber band
expand.

fascinating (FA suh naa ting)

Here's What It Means

adjective: attracting strong attention

Synonyms—*They have nearly the same meaning.*

appealing
attention-grabbing
charming
delightful
engaging
exciting
very interesting

Forms of *fascinating* to Share with 4s

fascinate (verb)
fascinates (verb)
fascinated (verb, adjective)
fascination (noun)

Talk & Share

1. This is a fascinating book!

2. My family was fascinated when I told my story.

3. So what is outside that seems to be fascinating everyone?

4. I was fascinated with a song I heard on the radio.

5. Snow fascinates me.

6. My sister's college dormitory room fascinates me.

7. A full moon fascinates me.

8. The baby has a fascination with one toy right now.

9. Your good manners fascinated me!

10. It's fascinating to watch vegetables grow in a garden.

Focusing Talk:
Talking about Fascinating Things

Use the word *fascinate* as you tell children about something fascinating that you've seen in real life. Then invite children to follow your model to tell about real-life things that have fascinated them. Repeat the activity to tell about a book that was fascinating. This is a rich skill-building activity because it encourages discussion about real vs. make-believe; it also encourages fascination around books, both fiction and nonfiction.

Hands-On:
Comparing Ideas that Fascinate

Provide enticing age-appropriate pictures for partners to identify *one* picture that fascinates *both* children. Repeat and then have children change partners. Help children notice how two people's opinions may differ around what is fascinating. You might extend the activity to talk about why people might like to have choices in books, movies, pets, toys, games, clothes, foods, and so on.

WOW! Rhyme: *fascinating*

I was fascinated
when I climbed the tree
'cause things on the ground
looked tiny to me.

Here's What It Means

adjective: easily damaged or broken

Synonyms—*They have nearly the same meaning.*

ailing	dainty
breakable	delicate
brittle	frail

Talk & Share

1. A glass mirror is fragile, so it might crack if I drop it.

2. It's important to hold fragile things very carefully.

3. My art project is fragile, so I won't fold it.

4. Dad's watch has fragile parts that are protected by the face plate.

5. Eyelids protect eyes, which are fragile.

6. I am careful when I touch my mother's fragile dishes.

7. A new baby seems really fragile.

8. I am sad, so my feelings are fragile right now.

9. Someone broke the figurine's fragile leg.

10. Would you be careful with this if I told you it's fragile?

Focusing Talk:
Focusing on Fragile Things

Present pictured or actual fragile items, such as eyeglasses, a toothpick sculpture, model airplane, origami art, figurines, glass container, ceramic bowl, mirror, clay sculpture, or an antique piece. Talk about perceived qualities that can cause each item to be considered fragile. In a community circle, discuss protective ways to handle or display each item. Children might draw or cut out pictures to create a group book titled "Fragile Things."

Hands-On:
Making Fragile Snowflakes

Talk about how a snowflake is fragile because it is tiny and melts very quickly. Help children make fragile paper snowflakes: Fold a paper square in half, and again in half. Hold at the corner as you fold to create a cone shape. Continue to fold until the cone shape can no longer be folded. Cut off a tiny piece at the point. On the folded edge, make several tiny cut-outs. All cuts should go through all thicknesses. Unfold…and behold!

WOW! Rhyme: **fragile**

It's fragile.

I'm careful.

I don't want to break it.

It's fragile.

I'm careful.

I won't drop or shake it!

Here's What It Means

adverb: right away

Synonyms—*They have nearly the same meaning.*

as soon as possible   quickly
instantly   right now
promptly   without delay

Figuratively Speaking

in the blink of an eye; rush right in; in a jiffy

Form of *immediately* to Share with 4s

immediate (adjective)

Talk & Share

1. I'd like that to happen immediately!

2. He called home immediately.

3. I jumped out of bed immediately when my alarm rang.

4. The phone rang immediately as I walked in.

5. She left immediately so we didn't get to play long.

6. An injury requires immediate attention.

7. When Earth started to shake, the clock stopped immediately.

8. My immediate need is for a drink of water.

9. Should we begin to follow that rule immediately?

10. I like it when we get to freeze immediately, like statues.

Focusing Talk:
Discussing Actions and Immediate Reactions

Help children name situations in which one action can cause an immediate reaction. Examples might include: something comes near an eye and causes the eyelid to blink; an unfamiliar noise causes an animal to scurry off; a triggered switch causes a light to go on or off; letting go of an item causes it to fall to the floor; removing a battery causes a device to stop working; and so on.

Hands-On:
Identifying Immediate Help

Talk about how a bowl offers immediate help as popcorn flows from an air popper or a bandage offers prompt help for a cut. Have partners cut out a pictured item, such as a vacuum, fire engine, ambulance, mop, ice pack, police car, or phone, that could offer immediate help in particular situations. Invite partners to dramatize a situation that is related to their pictured item. Encourage interchangeable use of *immediately, quickly,* and *promptly.*

WOW! Rhyme: ***immediately***

She made an immediate mess.
She did.
She emptied the trash,
then immediately hid.

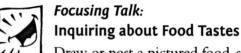
Here's What It Means

verb: to ask about

Synonyms—*They have nearly the same meaning.*

look into   seek

question   search out

scout

Figuratively Speaking

get the scoop on; dig out; grill

Forms of *inquire* to Share with 4s

inquired (verb)

inquires (verb)

inquiries (noun)

inquiring (adjective; verb)

inquiry (noun)

inquisitive (adjective)

Talk & Share

1. We will inquire to find out what time the play begins.

2. My teacher says we have inquiring minds!

3. Grandmom suggested we should be inquisitive and just inquire.

4. No one inquired about the author's name.

5. We had to inquire three times to get the right address.

6. A reporter inquires to gain information.

7. We made many inquiries for our survey.

8. My dog gets inquisitive when she smells food.

9. I made an inquiry and found a great playmate.

10. Dad was inquiring to learn my favorite book character.

Focusing Talk:
Inquiring about Food Tastes

Draw or post a pictured food, such as a sweet potato, and write its name on chart paper. Then draw around your spread hand, and count five fingers aloud. Model inquiring of five persons: "[name], do you like sweet potatoes?" Shade one drawn finger for each "yes" response. Then count aloud the shaded fingers to report the results of your inquiries. Help partners make and report on five similar inquiries about a food.

Hands-On:
Making Inquiries of Inquisitive Minds

Provide each child several bookmark strips that include the child's name. Children might illustrate bookmarks. Display an unfamiliar book and ask, "Who feels inquisitive about this book, and why?" Help children respond, "I feel inquisitive because… " before placing one of their personalized bookmarks in the book. Invite children to choose unfamiliar books and lead inquiries. Such inquisitive results may help select future read-alouds.

WOW! Rhyme: *inquire*

I have an inquisitive mind.

I inquire when I need to find

the address of a friend

or what's needing a mend…

I'm inquiring: Did I act unkind?

Here's What It Means

verb: to stop something

Synonyms—*They have nearly the same meaning.*

break in   halt
butt in   interfere
end   stop

Forms of *interrupt* to Share with 4s

interruption (noun)
interrupted (verb, adjective)
interrupts (verb)
interrupting (verb, adjective)

Talk & Share

1. Please don't interrupt me when I'm talking.

2. I didn't like the first interruption, nor the next five interruptions!

3. Excuse me for interrupting your play.

4. A phone call interrupted our dinner.

5. My trip to school was interrupted when our car ran out of gas.

6. My dog licked my hand and interrupted my nap!

7. My alarm clock often interrupts a really good dream.

8. Dad tells us we must not interrupt.

9. She says interrupting is rude.

10. Mom called on her cell phone, but another call interrupted our conversation.

Focusing Talk:
Identifying Interruptions

Invite children to name times when they do not want to be interrupted. For ideas, such as playing or talking, list heading words to tally children's thoughts. Or discuss and tally activities when someone might wish to be interrupted. Examples may include eating certain foods, going to bed, or doing chores. Have children enlist help at home to name common interruptions. Try inviting a talker to hold a "talking stick" as others listen.

Hands-On:
Interrupting Sips

Provide a straw and cup of water for each child. Help children experiment to find the extent to which bending of the straw interrupts their success in sipping water. Children will likely relate this activity to times they've seen water sprays interrupted when a sprinkler or water hose is bent or twisted. Help children name other interruptions, such as a power outage or phone call, that can cause someone to have to end an activity.

WOW! Rhyme: **interrupt**

Interruptions!
Interruptions!
Interruptions bother me.
Unless, of course, *I* am the one
who's interrupting...
see?

Here's What It Means

adjective: of a huge size

Another meaning:

(noun) an extinct relative of the elephant

Synonyms—_They have nearly the same meaning._

enormous	king sized
gigantic	very big
jumbo	very large

Talk & Share

1. I probably look mammoth to a bug.

2. I am not mammoth, but I wear big shoes.

3. My hand looks mammoth compared to our baby's hand.

4. This store has a mammoth parking lot.

5. My sister and I had a mammoth number of leaves to rake.

6. I have a mammoth problem.

7. Elephants seem like mammoth animals to me.

8. Grandpa does mammoth amounts of work.

9. Mom made a mammoth pan of popcorn.

10. I'd love a mammoth drink of water.

Focusing Talk:
Handling a Mammoth Problem

Tell children about a time you experienced a problem that felt mammoth to you. An example might be having to drive a long way when you were very tired or a time when you had a big job to do and little time to get it done. Talk about how you rested, began singing, thought happy thoughts, or counted so that you could feel less stressed. Invite children to name problems that seemed mammoth and tell how they helped to feel less stressed.

Hands-On:
Identifying Mammoth Things

Invite each child to wad up tissue paper or scrap paper to make balls of all sizes from tiny to very large. Then have children arrange the paper balls from smallest to largest. Encourage use of complete sentences with _mammoth_ and its synonyms as children talk about how a small paper ball might be compared to a far larger paper ball. At another time, help children identify pictures of mammoth animals, statues, or buildings.

WOW! Rhyme: **mammoth**

Mammoth!

It was mammoth!

It seemed bigger than a horse.

We made a mammoth pizza pie.

It fed us all, of course.

Here's What It Means

noun or adjective: the largest amount possible

Synonyms—*They have nearly the same meaning.*

greatest   largest

highest   to the limit

Figuratively Speaking

to the max

Forms of *maximum* to Share with 4s

maximize (verb)

maximizes (verb)

maximized (verb)

maximizing (verb)

Talk & Share

1. We can seat a maximum of four persons at this table.

2. We have already maximized the size of this balloon.

3. The maximum speed limit on this street is 25 miles per hour.

4. Many drivers don't stay under the maximum speed limit.

5. I am taller than the maximum height allowed for most rides at the park.

6. We can maximize the fun and spend less money.

7. The printer holds a maximum of one package of paper.

8. We are maximizing our play time.

9. Having company sometimes maximizes the time we get to stay up.

10. This game is for a maximum of four players.

Focusing Talk: Finding the Maximum

Talk about road signs on streets and highways that state the maximum speed within the law. Ask family members to help children write the numbers they spot on speed limit signs over a period of a few days. Have family members note where each sign was spotted. With your help, children will enjoy sharing their sightings with the class. Note: Children will find it fun to learn ways to use the descriptive phrase "...to the max."

Hands-On: Building to the Maximum

Provide building blocks for children to explore the maximum height one can build a single stack of blocks as compared to a structure with a larger foundation. Then invite children to compare various containers for the maximum number of blocks each can hold. Try containers, such as a bucket, pencil case, cottage cheese tub, shoe box, and an assortment of cardboard boxes. Invite children to share their findings in a community circle.

WOW! Rhyme: *maximum*

I want the max.

The maximum.

I want the maximum size.

I want to have the most of all.

I'll win the maximum prize.

Here's What It Means

noun or adjective: least

Synonyms—*They have nearly the same meaning.*

fewest
least

Forms of *minimum* to Share with 4s

minimal (adjective)
minimize (verb)

Talk & Share

1. This small table might minimize the size of our group.

2. I need a minimum of two people to help.

3. This will take a minimal amount of time.

4. I get to have a minimum of two friends come to play.

5. Our kite needs a minimum of two of us to fly it.

6. Mom says that, at the minimum, I must finish high school.

7. We keep our refrigerator at the minimum temperature.

8. We'd need to have a minimum of four parents come to help.

9. The animal shelter should have a minimum of five dogs, I'd think.

10. We can try to minimize the noise.

Focusing Talk: Discussing Minimums

Ask children to name the minimum number of players it takes to play checkers or hopscotch or marbles. How about jump rope or jacks? Then talk about the minimum number it takes to watch TV, read a book, or play a particular video game. Discuss why one person could not play checkers, while one person might play catch. Invite discussion of other games, such as football or soccer, that generally call for a larger minimum number of players.

Hands-On: Minimizing Sizes and Spaces

Provide assorted lengths of string, ribbon, chenille sticks, and similar pliable materials for partners to experiment in making circles or ovals and comparing their sizes. Have children lay out on paper the largest closed shape their length of paper allows, and then draw around it. Have children minimize their shape—make it the smallest it can be—and draw around it. Children may choose to compare sizes and shapes by laying a smaller shape inside of a larger shape.

WOW! Rhyme: **minimum**

This is the minimum.
This is the least.
This is the minimum
food for a feast.

Here's What It Means

adjective: puzzling

Synonyms—They have nearly the same meaning.

secretive
unknown

Forms of *mysterious* to Share with 4s

mysteriously (adverb)
mystery (noun)

Talk & Share

1. There was a mysterious smell in the sink.

2. I like mystery stories.

3. Mom said I was mysteriously quiet.

4. No one knows the answer to this mysterious question.

5. Didn't you think it was mysterious?

6. It was a mystery how my shirt got covered with sand.

7. I looked everywhere and it's still a mystery to me.

8. I've never seen anything that looked as mysterious as that does.

9. We had a mysterious water leak.

10. The mound of dirt in the yard was mysteriously shrinking each day.

Focusing Talk:
Discussing Mysterious Mysteries

Tell children about something that seemed mysterious to you. An example may be a shoe that suddenly came up missing when you were certain you'd just seen both shoes. Talk about how you tried to solve the mystery and whether or not you solved it. Then invite children to follow your model, using *mystery* and its forms, to name a mystery, to tell how they tried to solve it, and to say whether or not their mysterious mystery is still a mystery.

Hands-On:
Discovering Mysterious Wishes

Using old catalogs, help children cut out pictured items they wish they could own and glue the pictures on sheets of paper. Show children how to hide a wished-for item by laying a second paper on top. Staple the two papers across the top, and help children write "(child's name)'s Mystery Wish" on the top paper. Collect and redistribute the Mystery Wishes for children to discover each friend's "Mysterious Wish."

WOW! Rhyme: **mysterious**

It's all wrapped up.
It's in a box.
I don't know what's inside.
A present is mysterious.
Its wrapping lets it hide.

Here's What It Means

adjective: many

Synonyms—*They have nearly the same meaning.*

a lot of

lots

Figuratively Speaking

oodles; oodles and gobs; gobs; like leaves in a forest

Talk & Share

1. We could have numerous pets in our room.

2. There are numerous colleges I could attend when I am older.

3. My sister has numerous chores.

4. We have numerous rules at my house.

5. I like numerous foods.

6. We read in numerous books about animals.

7. I looked numerous places until I found my book.

8. We had numerous choices at lunch today.

9. My uncle has traveled to numerous states.

10. I wash my hands numerous times each day.

Focusing Talk:
Noting Numerous Ways to Travel

Designate two places that are across the room from one another. Talk about your choice of one of numerous ways to travel—such as boat, plane, car, truck, bike, and so on—as you move from one point to the other. Use position words, such as *around, in front of, behind,* or *across,* as you describe your pretend journey. Have volunteers "travel," discussing the numerous means of travel, their choice, and why they chose that mode.

Hands-On:
Sorting Numerous Shapes

Read "Circles" (see Resources, page 176). Provide numerous paper cut-outs of squares, circles, triangles, and rectangles. Invite children to watch you draw one shape on each of four sheets of paper. Talk about each shape as you draw. Help children count a shape's corners and line segments, and note the circle's difference. Then have children match all the cut-out circles to the circle sheet, triangles to the triangle, and so on.

WOW! Rhyme: **numerous**

I do lots of things
in lots of ways
at numerous times
on numerous days!

Here's What It Means

noun: what someone thinks

Synonyms—*They have nearly the same meaning.*

attitude	my idea about
belief	my own thought
judgment	viewpoint

Figuratively Speaking

two cents' worth

Form of *opinion* to Share with 4s

opinionated (adjective)

Talk & Share

1. I think we should hear everyone's opinions.

2. Is anyone able to listen without being opinionated?

3. My dad listens to my opinions.

4. It's my opinion that we should eat pizza every night!

5. I'd like your opinion of this new rule.

6. My mom says I'm opinionated when it comes to my hair.

7. It makes things easy when our opinions are the same.

8. Our opinions are different because we are different people.

9. My opinion is that different people can like different things.

10. In my opinion, it's too cold in here.

Focusing Talk: Comparing Opinions

Ask children's preferences for such things as hot or cold food, hot or cold drinks, red or blue colors, jeans or sweatpants, tied shoes or sandals, school or weekend days, morning or evening, plump or thin bed pillows, a dog or a cat for a household pet, and so on. If children tend to change their opinions to go with the crowd, talk about the importance of having one's own unique opinion. Tally and discuss the results. How do opinions vary?

Hands-On: Tallying Opinions

Provide paper for each child to draw around one hand with fingers spread. Have children cut out and glue a magazine picture onto the other side of the paper. Tell children to ask for opinions about their picture from five different people. Have children draw on the back of their picture one fingernail on one finger for each person's opinion they gain. Invite children to share surveyed opinions in a community circle.

WOW! Rhyme: **opinion**

Your opinion
is how you feel.
And my opinion is mine.
And whether they're different
or nearly the same,
Both our opinions are fine.

participate (par TI suh paat)

Here's What It Means

verb: to join in

Synonyms—*They have nearly the same meaning.*

play with   take part in

share in   work with

Forms of *participate* to Share with 4s

participant (noun)

participation (noun)

Talk & Share

1. We hope you will participate in this game.

2. Mom asked for my participation.

3. I tried to participate several times.

4. I don't know how, so I can't participate.

5. Come on! We need more participants.

6. I volunteered to participate.

7. No one would participate.

8. I need help, so I hope you'll participate.

9. I will participate in your group.

10. My group has three participants.

Focusing Talk:
Talking about Participation

Model talking and writing about an activity in which you like to participate. For example, write, "I like to dance." as you say, "I like to participate in dancing." Invite children to use the word *participate* and its forms as they tell about activities they like to do. At another time, help children talk about activities in which they prefer not to participate. Encourage sentences, such as "I don't like to be a participant in (activity)."

Hands-On:
Participating to Create a Collage

Provide old magazines and a large sheet of paper for children to create five or six collages with different themes. Invite children to participate in naming each theme. Themes may be: wild animals, kitchen items, people, foods, trees and plants, alphabet letters, numbers, things that make music, and so on. Ask children to be participants in each collage by either contributing a picture or helping to glue on a picture another participant shares.

WOW! Rhyme: *participate*

It's easy to participate,

'cause all I need to do

is offer to help whenever I can,

and I will be helping you.

Here's What It Means

adjective: sure; certain

Synonyms—*They have nearly the same meaning.*

absolutely   yes

no doubt   optimistic

Figuratively Speaking

a rosy outlook; paint a rosy picture

Form of *positive* to Share with 4s

positively (adverb)

Talk & Share

1. Are you positive you feel okay?

2. I am positive I can do this.

3. Positively no one knows about this.

4. This is positively the best sandwich!

5. I'll go with you if you're positive it's okay.

6. I positively do not like turnips.

7. I'm positive this song is my favorite.

8. Was Grandpa positive he heard me?

9. The dog's barking is a positive sign there's someone here.

10. Are they positive it's going to snow?

Focusing Talk:
Identifying What's Positively True

To encourage children to say, "It's positively true!", share true statements, such as "Apples grow on trees," "Some trees lose their leaves in the winter," or "We live on the planet Earth." Include several untrue statements, such as "All people know how to swim," "Fingernails don't grow," or "A lemon tastes sweet." Encourage children to lead the group for others to use sentences to identify statements as positively true or not.

Hands-On:
Being Positively Artistic

Talk about how positive statements are helpful or kind. Then model making a plus sign as you say a positive statement, such as "Come play with us," or "I will share my crayons with you." Continue until the paper is covered with + signs such that it appears to be a work of art. Provide paper and markers and invite partners to take turns talking and drawing + signs to create *positively* artful masterpieces.

WOW! Rhyme: *positive*

Did Humpty Dumpty fall off the wall?

It's positively true.

Did Jack and Jill fall down the hill?

It's positively true.

It's true. It is. I know it's true.

I've heard those tales.

Have you?

Have you?

(*Note:* You may want to share "Alas!," "Humpty Dumpty," and "Squirmy Earthworm." See Resources, pages 175, 177, 181.)

predicament (pree DIK uh muhnt)

Here's What It Means

noun: difficult or puzzling situation

Synonyms—*They have nearly the same meaning.*

big problem
bind
tough time

Figuratively Speaking

a fine kettle of fish; in a stew;
a fine how-do-you-do

Talk & Share

1. I was in a predicament when I couldn't find my toothbrush.

2. Our predicament was solved when we untangled the rope.

3. Losing one shoe put me in a predicament.

4. My dad was in a predicament when he ran out of gas.

5. A predicament is a difficult situation.

6. Gum in my hair caused a real predicament.

7. We had a predicament when we lost the map.

8. It's a predicament to find our way in the dark.

9. If he finds himself in a predicament, he can call for help.

10. Mom thinks we might help her solve a predicament.

Focusing Talk:
Thinking Through a Predicament

Read and discuss "Bunny Rabbit's Predicament" (see Resources, page 176). Talk about ideas for resolving other kinds of predicaments, such as being locked out of your home or car, having gum stuck to a shoe or candle wax or gum stuck to clothing, being cold with no jacket nearby, or having a lollipop's stickiness all over your hands. Encourage all ideas, and then try some ideas as time allows.

Hands-On:
Making a Book about Predicaments

Provide magazines and newspapers for partners to cut out a picture depicting a predicament. Some children may prefer to draw pictures. Have children glue pictures onto separate pages to contribute to a book titled "What a Predicament!" Write a sentence or two as each child tells his or her picture's story and suggests a way to resolve the predicament. Bind the pages and invite children to take turns sharing the book with family members.

WOW! Rhyme: **predicament**

What a predicament!
What'll I do?
My gum is stuck!
It's stuck to my shoe!

Here's What It Means

verb: to say that something might happen in the future

Synonyms—*They have nearly the same meaning.*

expect to happen

share opinion about what might happen

Forms of *predict* to Share with 4s

prediction (noun)

predictions (noun)

predictable (adjective)

predicting (verb)

predicts (verb)

predicted (verb)

Talk & Share

1. Was rain predicted today?

2. It's hard to predict what will happen.

3. We make predictions all the time.

4. Why do you predict I'll be cold?

5. I predicted my dog would bark when she heard you.

6. Are you predicting how many will come to the party?

7. My dad thinks snow is predictable today.

8. Mom predicts I'll be really tall when I go to college.

9. Who'll make a prediction before we open the box?

10. I can't predict what my mom might say.

Focusing Talk: Predicting What Will Happen

Lay a crayon on a table's edge. Ask children to predict what might happen if the table were bumped. (The crayon might roll and fall off.) Suggest more predictable scenarios, such as overfilling a cup, holding open scissors near paper or skin, observing dark clouds, or stacking blocks too high. Encourage children to begin each of their predictions by saying, "I predict…," "It's predictable that…," or "My prediction is that…."

Hands-On: Predicting the Weather

Share "Rainbow Colors" (see Resources, page 180). Talk about rainbows, which appear when there are rain and sunshine at the same time. Provide glue, cotton balls, colored paper, and crayons or pieces of chenille sticks in a rainbow's seven colors (red, orange, yellow, green, blue, indigo, violet). Help children cut or tear paper and use other materials to depict a sky that predicts rain or one that predicts or shows a rainbow.

WOW! Rhyme: *predict*

I predicted all of my blocks might fall
if anyone added another.
But who could predict the blocks
    would fall
on top of me and my brother!

Here's What It Means

verb: to suggest an idea

Synonyms—*They have nearly the same meaning.*

come up with   plan

offer   present an idea

Forms of *propose* to Share with 4s

proposal (noun)

proposed (verb)

proposition (noun)

Talk & Share

1. I propose that we share.

2. Hey, I want to propose a fun idea!

3. Does your proposal include everyone?

4. Will you consider a proposition?

5. My proposition is that we all go out to play.

6. Let's propose that idea to the others.

7. Does anyone have a book to propose?

8. I proposed that we have pizza for dinner.

9. We have two proposals to consider.

10. Who has another idea to propose?

Focusing Talk: Proposing Ideas

Invite children to propose specific ways to show kindness. Proposed ideas might include: not hitting, asking someone to play, helping find a lost item, rescue lost or homeless animals, recycle items to help the planet, or speaking kind words. Encourage children to begin their suggestions with words such as "I propose that…," "My proposal is that…," or "I have a proposition that…."

Hands-On: Proposing Improvements

Help children think about ways to improve their community. Provide old newspapers and magazines for children to cut out pictures to create a book. Help children select pictures of items, such as a pool, trash can, picnic table, park, and so on. Write as children dictate proposals, such as put trash in can, clean off table, take trash out of pool, and so on. Have children sign their pages. Add a title page, along with a page to index the book by author.

WOW! Rhyme: *propose*

I propose you do it.

And here's my reason why.

I propose you do it.

If not,

I'm gonna cry.

Here's What It Means

verb: to know as familiar

Synonyms—*They have nearly the same meaning.*

catch on   notice
get the idea   realize
give attention to   understand

Figuratively Speaking

see the light

Forms of *recognize* to Share with 4s

recognition (noun)
recognized (verb)
recognizes (verb)
recognizing (verb)

Talk & Share

1. Does anyone recognize that dog?

2. I didn't recognize you in that costume.

3. My mom always recognizes my voice.

4. We recognized their car.

5. I recognized your eagerness to help.

6. He earned recognition for doing a good job.

7. You might recognize my brother when you see him.

8. Who recognizes where this puzzle piece goes?

9. I hope someone is recognizing how hard I have tried.

10. Who can recognize a map of the United States?

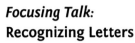

Focusing Talk:
Recognizing Letters

Provide old newspapers and magazines, along with alphabet letters. Invite children to choose an alphabet letter they recognize and then comb newspaper or magazine pages to find and match that letter. Ask children to show the two matching letters as they say, "I recognize these letters. They are both (letter's name)." Repeat for children to make numerous matches from print for one or more alphabet letters in their first names.

Hands-On:
Recognizing Members of a Family

Invite children to bring in pictures of themselves and family members. Have children work in small groups to scramble their family photos and then work to recognize and sort the group's pictures into each child's correct family groups. Help children recognize that family members often resemble one another. Before beginning this activity, you'll want to code the back of each picture to avoid mix-ups and to help children check their own work.

WOW! Rhyme: **recognize**

When we look in a mirror—
Who is it we see?
Do you recognize you?
Do you recognize me?

Here's What It Means

adjective: very silly; laughable

Synonyms—*They have nearly the same meaning.*

foolish   makes no sense
goofy   nonsense

Figuratively Speaking

hogwash

Form of *ridiculous* to Share with 4s

ridiculously (adverb)

Talk & Share

1. I saw a ridiculous show on TV.
2. This costume looks ridiculous.
3. Mom thinks her haircut is ridiculously short.
4. Some people think computers are ridiculous.
5. Who knows the ridiculous words to that song?
6. It's a ridiculous way to get attention.
7. Dad had to work ridiculous hours on the weekend.
8. It's ridiculous that this chalk keeps breaking.
9. I like that ridiculous poem.
10. Let's say some ridiculous words.

Focusing Talk: Saying Ridiculous Things

On a map of the United States, point to your approximate location as you say, "We are here in (location)." Prepare to use your other hand to point to a faraway city on the map as you say, "I know we are here in (actual location), so it would be ridiculous to say we are there in (finger on different city)." Repeat for other location comparisons. Then invite children to follow your sentence model to make similar comparisons on the map.

Hands-On: Illustrating Ridiculous Ideas

Share a Mary Poppins story and the poem "A Stupid Feud" (see Resources, page 181). Help children draw from life experiences and from stories they know to name a ridiculous idea, such as walking on a ceiling or a dog walking a human on a leash. Using a simple sentence, write each idea as a caption on drawing paper. Have children draw or cut out pictures to illustrate each idea. Repeat the activity often and collate ideas for a class book.

WOW! Rhyme: *ridiculous*

It's ridiculous what he has said.
He's said he's forgotten his head.
But his head is right there.
Yep, it's under his hair.
How silly! He *must* go to bed!

Here's What It Means

adjective: questioning for truth

Synonyms—*They have nearly the same meaning.*

distrusting
doubtful

Figuratively Speaking

smell a rat

Forms of *suspicious* to Share with 4s

suspect (noun, verb)
suspects (verb)
suspected (verb)
suspicion (noun)

Talk & Share

1. I was suspicious when the door opened.

2. A few clues led the policewoman to name a suspect.

3. We heard some suspicious noises.

4. Do you suspect something's wrong?

5. I suspected you would be suspicious!

6. Dad was not at all suspicious, so we surprised him.

7. I had a sneaky suspicion that you were behind me!

8. This may cause Grandpa to be suspicious.

9. The missing candy caused some suspicions.

10. I promise to tell you if I see anything suspicious.

Focusing Talk:
Feeling Suspicious

Using complete sentences, tell children about a time when you felt suspicious about a situation and why. You might include characters whom you felt were possible suspects who'd caused something to happen or not happen. An example might be: "I felt suspicious when I noticed a cookie was missing. I saw the dog running away." Help children follow your model to tell of situations when they felt suspicious and why.

Hands-On:
Making Suspicious-looking Characters

Provide various shapes cut from colored cardstock, along with scissors, glue, and construction materials, such as chenille sticks, cotton balls, craft sticks, bubble wrap, popcorn packing, bottle caps, and cardboard tubes. Invite partners to create suspicious-looking characters. Encourage children to share their characters in a community circle and invite classmates to tell why each character might arouse someone's suspicions.

WOW! Rhyme: *suspicious*

If there's something suspicious about it,
And it doesn't seem right—
Then I'd doubt it.

Here's What It Means

adjective: kind; full of thought

Synonyms—*They have nearly the same meaning.*

considerate
helpful

Form of *thoughtful* to Share with 4s

thoughtfully (adverb)

Talk & Share

1. It's thoughtful of you to come with me.

2. No one was being thoughtful.

3. I try to be thoughtful when someone is hurt.

4. Grammy likes it when I am thoughtful.

5. It's thoughtful to be quiet when someone is sleeping.

6. I need to act more thoughtfully than I did just now.

7. I was thoughtful to include everyone in the game.

8. I like it when my friends act thoughtfully and include me.

9. Well, that was a thoughtful thing to say. Thank you!

10. My mom thanked me for my thoughtful card to her.

Focusing Talk: Being Thoughtful

Help children name times when they have noticed someone who acted thoughtfully to another person. An example might be when a child moves over so another person can sit down or see what's happening. List children's ideas in short sentences, such as "It was thoughtful of Bennie to share his grapes." Ask partners to dramatize thoughtful actions from the list. Encourage family members to look for extensions of this activity at home!

Hands-On: Giving Thoughtful Thanks

Provide folded cardstock for each child to illustrate the inside of a "Thoughtful Thanks" card to thank a family member for a thoughtful action. Ideas may include gratitude for a trip to a park or play date, a favorite meal, or help with shampooing hair. You may want to help children draw around one hand on the card front and the other hand on the back. Invite children to write their names on their cards.

Thoughtful Thanks

WOW! Rhyme: *thoughtful*

It's good to be thoughtful.
It's good to be kind.
It's good to help out
when a friend's in a bind.

Here's What It Means

adjective: right now

Synonyms—*They have nearly the same meaning.*

can't wait
emergency
immediate need

Forms of *urgent* to Share with 4s

urgency (noun)
urgently (adverb)

Figuratively Speaking

ASAP (as soon as possible)

Talk & Share

1. Please hurry! This is urgent!
2. This is urgent and cannot wait.
3. There's really no urgency.
4. It isn't urgent, but please do this as soon as you can.
5. Mom received an urgent phone call.
6. My cat seemed to need urgent attention.
7. It's urgent that we get help for that raccoon with the jar on his head.
8. A fire truck raced urgently down our street.
9. It's urgent that I find my friend.
10. A cut needs urgent care.

Focusing Talk:
Identifying Urgencies

Read "The Boy Who Cried Wolf" ("The Shepherd Boy and the Wolf"; see Resources, page 174). Discuss why fear of something, like a wolf, would cause a need for urgent help. Ask why no one paid attention to the boy the first time he cried for help. Help children name and tell reasons for urgencies, such as going to the bathroom, grabbing a cup that's about to spill, or moving a vehicle out of the way for emergency vehicles.

Hands-On:
Providing Urgent Care

Provide scissors, glue, and old magazines and newspapers. You might also provide packaging from first aid supplies or pictured red crosses that signify medical assistance. Help partners identify, cut out, and glue onto colored paper one pictured scene that suggests urgent care is required. Have children identify, cut out, and match pictures of first aid treatments or tools that might help the people or animals in the scene.

WOW! Rhyme: **urgent**

This is urgent, really urgent.
This is urgent.
Please come now!
I cannot turn the faucet off.
Please come and show me how.

Here's What It Means

adjective: worth a lot

Synonyms—*They have nearly the same meaning.*

cost a lot	treasured
meaningful	worthwhile
priceless	worthy
special	

Forms of *valuable* to Share with 4s

value (noun, verb)
valued (adjective, verb)

Talk & Share

1. My mom says I am valuable to her.
2. I value my cat.
3. This toy is valued highly by my friends.
4. I see valuable things in stores.
5. Some valued metals are gold and silver.
6. Mom says our neighbors value being able to drive.
7. Food, sleep, and exercise are valuable for my body.
8. Today I learned the value of believing in myself.
9. Grandpa says he values spending time with me!
10. My books are valuable to me.

Focusing Talk:
Discussing Values

Tell children about a person, place, or thing that is valuable to you and why you value it. Then invite children to talk about things they value and tell why. Help children notice how different people feel that some things, such as family, pets, toys, foods, saving energy or money, or recycling, are valuable, while people may not agree about the value of other things, such as time alone or waking up early. You may want to list and tally children's ideas to illustrate different values of different people.

Hands-On:
Comparing Valuable Items

Provide two pictured items for children to identify the item that would likely be more valuable, or cost more money. Compare items of very different costs, such as: shoes and car, pencil and house, cell phone and apple. Talk about why a car might not be valued if someone can't drive or how shoes lose value when they wear out or as feet grow. At another time, challenge children to compare the values of three or four pictured items.

WOW! Rhyme: **valuable**

I value me.

I value you.

I value things I get to do.

I get to eat.

I get to play.

My life is valuable every day!

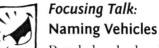

Here's What It Means

noun: a carrier of people or things

Synonyms—*some kinds of vehicles*

airplane	car
bicycle	train
bus	truck
boat	

Talk & Share

1. What vehicle can carry many people?

2. I like to ride in a vehicle that goes on tracks.

3. Some vehicles travel on land.

4. Some vehicles travel on water.

5. Some vehicles travel in the air.

6. This is my favorite vehicle.

7. What vehicle will take you home today?

8. We went across the river on a vehicle called a ferry.

9. A bicycle is a vehicle that has two wheels.

10. A tricycle is a vehicle that has three wheels.

Focusing Talk: Naming Vehicles

Read aloud a book or poem about vehicles, such as *Cars and Trucks and Things That Go, The Bridge Is Up!*, or *Sputter, Sputter, Sput!* (see Resources, page 173). Then say, "A motorcycle is a vehicle." Write *motorcycle* to begin a list on chart paper. Invite children to follow your oral sentence model to name many different types of vehicles. Help children include vehicles, such as a barge or boxcar, that generally carry things rather than people.

Hands-On: Sorting Vehicles

Provide pictures of vehicles, including some that are less common, such as an open-air tour bus, hot air balloon, raft, subway, or hydroplane. Invite partners to sort the pictured vehicles into those that travel by land, by air, and water. Have children take turns using the word *vehicle* to tell about each group. For example, "These vehicles all travel on land," or "These vehicles carry people and things across water."

WOW! Rhyme: **vehicle**

Some vehicles travel the roads.
Some vehicles travel the sea.
Some vehicles fly high,
way up in the sky.
And some vehicles travel with me!

AGE 5

- ☐ alert
- ☐ analyze
- ☐ anticipate
- ☐ appropriate
- ☐ astonished
- ☐ authority
- ☐ cautious
- ☐ conquer
- ☐ conserve
- ☐ consume
- ☐ cumbersome
- ☐ discourage
- ☐ distract
- ☐ enthusiastic
- ☐ error
- ☐ flexible
- ☐ frantic
- ☐ frequently

- ☐ ignore
- ☐ irritated
- ☐ obligation
- ☐ observe
- ☐ occasional
- ☐ original
- ☐ persuade
- ☐ prohibit
- ☐ realistic
- ☐ recommend
- ☐ remarkable
- ☐ resemble
- ☐ resume
- ☐ summarize
- ☐ threaten
- ☐ tremendous
- ☐ undoubtedly
- ☐ variety

Here's What It Means

adjective: to pay attention; to warn

noun: a warning

Synonyms—*They have nearly the same meaning.*

attentive   intelligent

awake   watchful

aware

Figuratively Speaking

on the ball; with it; all ears

Forms of *alert* to Share with 5s

alerted (verb)

alerting (verb)

alertly (adverb)

alertness (noun)

alerts (verb)

Talk & Share

1. I'm too tired to feel alert today.

2. I'll throw you the ball when you seem alert.

3. I see that you are sitting alertly.

4. His alertness helped him jump out of the way.

5. Dad acted alertly and noticed that I needed help.

6. Your yell alerted everyone to the danger.

7. Please alert the teacher about that broken table leg.

8. A loud buzzing alerts us to pay attention to weather alerts.

9. Our dog alerted us to the burglar.

10. The weather report says we have an ozone alert.

Focusing Talk: Sounding an Alert

Share "The Boy Who Cried Wolf" ("The Shepherd Boy and the Wolf") (see Resources, page 174) and "Bird Alert" (page 175). Play music for partners to dance, and then stop and stand alertly when the music stops. One child asks, "What's the alert?" as a partner responds with an alert, such as "Your cup could spill!" or "We have to go!" Invite children to offer alerts. Talk about how a vehicle with a loud siren alerts drivers to pull over and stop.

Hands-On: Acting Alert

Provide paper, newspapers, and magazines. Help each child draw a sign, symbol, or word that alerts and informs people. For example, children may draw an EXIT or STOP sign, a bathroom door's icon, or a red cross that notes the location of first aid equipment. Help children post their signs around the school or at home. At another time, have children draw or cut and paste pictures to illustrate people who are behaving alertly in particular situations.

WOW! Rhyme: **alert**

They almost bumped,

but neither got hurt

'cause both of my friends

were being alert.

Yeah!

Here's What It Means

verb: to study carefully in order to understand

Synonyms—*They have nearly the same meaning.*

examine   review

investigate   inspect

look at carefully

Forms of *analyze* to Share with 5s

analysis (noun)

analyst (noun)

analytical (adjective)

analytically (adverb)

analyzed (verb, adjective)

analyzes (verb)

analyzing (verb)

Talk & Share

1. Let's analyze this problem.

2. After doing your analysis, tell me if you think the toy will work.

3. We'll need an analyst to analyze the instructions before we begin.

4. The scientist handed the analyzed water to her assistant.

5. I often think analytically to find an answer.

6. Albert Einstein had an analytical mind.

7. She analyzes drawings to find hidden pictures.

8. My mama analyzed the job after I made my bed.

9. I washed my shirt after spilling on it and then analyzed it for stains.

10. After analyzing your plans, this project seems doable.

Focusing Talk:
Analyzing Alternative Uses of Items

Invite children to use their imaginations to consider creative uses for an item, such as a sheet of paper (shade eyes, funnel), a cup (trace around its rim to make a circle, hold pencils), or a piece of cardboard (roof, ramp). Have partners take turns sharing an idea for an item and why they think their idea is reasonable. Encourage listeners to ask questions.

Hands-On:
Thinking Analytically

Have children hold a marker in their writing hand, close their eyes, and feel around for a sheet of paper placed in front of them. Tell children to keep eyes closed and mark five dots anywhere on their paper. Invite children to open their eyes, analyze their dots, and then connect them in any manner to create a shape. Children might add details to create a recognizable picture. Repeat to mark, analyze, and connect more or fewer dots.

WOW! Rhyme: *analyze*

To understand it,

I analyze

with my brain

and my fingers,

my nose,

ears,

and eyes.

(And sometimes my mouth!)

Here's What It Means
verb: to think something will happen

Synonyms—*They have nearly the same meaning.*
count on   look ahead
expect   look forward to
guess   predict
hope for

Figuratively Speaking
get your hopes up; keep fingers crossed

Forms of *anticipate* to Share with 5s
anticipated (verb, adjective)
anticipates (verb)
anticipating (verb)
anticipation (noun)

Talk & Share
1. What do you anticipate doing this weekend?
2. I anticipated that you would say that.
3. He anticipates getting in trouble for the choice he made.
4. We're anticipating a delicious snack today.
5. I felt sad in anticipation of going home.
6. I anticipated seeing a large glob of ketchup come out of the bottle.
7. Those clouds mean we should anticipate rain soon.
8. The anticipated storm didn't arrive in our town!
9. I anticipate going to my dad's college when I get older.
10. We are filled with the anticipation of a fun vacation.

Focusing Talk: Anticipating Happenings
Read aloud a surprise-ending storybook, such as *Chicka Chicka Boom Boom, Stephanie's Ponytail, David's Father,* or *Each Peach Pear Plum* (see Resources, page 173). Stop often to ask what children *anticipate* might happen. Encourage responses in complete sentences that use anticipate and its forms. At another time, discuss what children anticipate they will be doing at this time tomorrow, at age ten, or when they reach another older age.

Hands-On: Building Anticipation
Have children fold paper in half and place the fold at the top. On the outside, children might draw or glue a picture of their own facial expression in anticipation of a scolding, opening a gift, or playing for a favorite college team. Help children draw on the inside a scene showing what might have caused that expression. Invite children to use *anticipate* as they tell their stories from beginning to end. Read "My Faces" (see Resources, page 179).

WOW! Rhyme: **anticipate**

I guess, expect,
and might predict
this present's what I'm hopin'.
BUT
anticipation tells me nothing
till my present's open!

Here's What It Means

adjective: right for the situation

Synonyms—*They have nearly the same meaning.*

acceptable	good
correct	proper
fitting	suitable

Forms of *appropriate* to Share with 5s

appropriately (adverb)

appropriateness (noun)

inappropriate (adjective)

inappropriately (adverb)

Talk & Share

1. You made an appropriate choice.

2. Do we have the appropriate number of chairs for everyone?

3. We need to dress appropriately for this weather.

4. It's appropriate to expect privacy in the bathroom.

5. Belching in public is inappropriate.

6. My little brother threw the ball inappropriately at first.

7. Rules that are appropriate help everyone have fun.

8. It is always appropriate to raise your hand if you want to talk.

9. I liked how you chose appropriate words even though you were angry.

10. It is inappropriate to draw on these walls.

Focusing Talk:
Recognizing Appropriate Behaviors

Help children list appropriate and inappropriate behaviors, such as grabbing someone's toy, wearing a heavy coat on a hot day, helping tie a shoe, laughing at someone's mistake, reading during quiet time, and so on. For each example, ask children to nod and say, "That's appropriate!" or shake heads and say, "That's inappropriate!" At another time, discuss feelings about various behaviors and ways to improve on inappropriate behaviors.

Hands-On:
Recording Appropriate Behaviors

Provide two half-sheets of paper for each child. Laying one sheet over the other, help children fold to create an eight-page book to include front and back covers. Staple along the fold. Help children draw a happy face and write their name on the cover. Ask children to look for appropriate behaviors and illustrate each on a page. Ask children to use *appropriate* and its forms in sentences to tell their stories. Repeat for books about inappropriate behaviors.

WOW! Rhyme: ***appropriate***

Appropriate is what appropriate does
unless it's not appropriate...
then—
Inappropriate is what inappropriate
   does...

Ah! We shall have none of that!

Here's What It Means

verb: to be amazed
adjective: amazed

Synonyms—*They have nearly the same meaning.*

amazed   shocked
astounded   stunned
flabbergasted   surprised

Figuratively Speaking

blown away; knocked off my feet; speechless

Forms of *astonished* to Share with 5s

astonish (verb)
astonishes (verb)
astonishing (adjective, verb)
astonishingly (adverb)
astonishment (noun)

Talk & Share

1. You seem to know astonishing facts about dinosaurs.
2. It's astonishing me to see how quickly you learn a song.
3. Did the magician's trick astonish you?
4. The doctor was astonished at how much I'd grown.
5. I saw Mom's astonishment when I tied my own shoes.
6. My dog empties her food bowl astonishingly fast.
7. My little brother astonishes me with his big words.
8. My dad says he's astonished when I recite a whole book.
9. Our fire alarm is astonishingly loud.
10. My cousin Nunie can write an astonishing number of words.

Focusing Talk:
Telling an Astonishing Tale

Explain that you need children's help to recite a poem. Tell children that as they listen, they will know when to speak and show astonishment with wide eyes and open mouth. Read aloud the poem "My True Story" (see Resources, page 179), pausing as words invite children to respond. Ask children to tell their feelings as they listen to each new detail in the poem. Have children use *astonish* and its forms to retell the poem's story.

Hands-On:
Making Pop-ups to Astonish Folks

Provide each child with a craft stick, a 3-inch paper square, and two egg-shaped paper cutouts that are 4 inches tall and whose long edges have been glued together to leave an opening from top to bottom. Invite children to decorate the front and back side of each egg shape. Have children draw an "astonishing-looking creature" on the 3-inch square, glue it to the craft stick, and slip it through the paper egg's opening to have the creature appear to be popping up and down.

WOW! Rhyme: **astonished**

I was astonished to see my dog
go hop-hop-hopping—
hopping over a log.
But I was far more astonished
when my hop-hopping dog
went hop-hopping off...
with a hop-hopping frog!

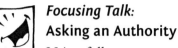

Here's What It Means

noun: a person who knows a lot about a certain subject

Another meaning:

noun: the power to act or give orders

Synonyms—*They have nearly the same meaning.*

boss   expert
command   master
control   specialist
creator

Figuratively Speaking

chief; ruler of the roost; in the driver's seat

Forms of *authority* to Share with 5s

author (noun)
authorities (noun)
authorize (verb)
authorizes (verb)
authorized (verb)
authors (noun)

Talk & Share

1. Our librarian is an authority on good books.

2. My teacher helped us to be authors.

3. Joseph will authorize the care of his caterpillar.

4. This paper authorizes you to walk in the halls.

5. You sound like an author, because you are quite an authority on healthy foods.

6. I need to act with authority so the others will listen.

7. This note appears to give you the authority to go with us.

8. My bus driver reports kind behavior to authorities also.

9. Sammy is an authority on insects because she has studied them.

10. My parents authorized the party plans, so we can send invitations.

Focusing Talk: Asking an Authority

Using full sentences, tell children your name and that you consider yourself an authority on a task, such as how to find a book's index or how to fold a paper in half. Then talk authoritatively as you perform that task. Invite questions about your performance before having children take turns to follow your model. Continue for children to share their authoritative knowledge about how to tie a shoe, feed a dog, or set a table for two persons.

Hands-On: Writing Authoritatively

Help children explore the outside and inside covers of several nonfiction books. Explain that an author who writes a nonfiction book is considered an authority who knows a lot about that topic and writes to teach others. Provide blank booklets (paper folded across the width and stapled on the fold) and help partners write and/or illustrate authoritatively on a topic they both know well. Display books as "Authoritative Works."

WOW! Rhyme: **authority**

**I don't know how to do it
so I'll find a book to read.
An author with authority
might give the help I need.**

Here's What It Means

adjective: careful

Synonyms—*They have nearly the same meaning.*

alert   careful
attentive   watchful

Figuratively Speaking

test the water

Forms of *cautious* to Share with 5s

caution (noun, verb)
cautioned (verb)
cautioning (verb)
cautions (verb)
cautiously (adverb)

Talk & Share

1. I walk cautiously when I carry dishes to the sink.

2. Did you see the caution sign by the big hole?

3. I am being cautious as I put this block on the tower.

4. My moms are always cautioning me to look both ways at the street corner.

5. The teacher cautioned us to avoid puddles on the playground.

6. I touch our pet tarantula cautiously.

7. She cautions her baby brother so he won't fall.

8. Dad said to use caution when we hammer the nails.

9. He was cautious as he walked across the wet floor.

10. The police officer told Uncle Shae to drive more cautiously.

Focusing Talk: Following Cautiously

Ask children to follow you in a line and echo your words and actions as you substitute "walking" and "walk" in "Standing Tall" (see Resources, page 181) to sing "Walking Tall." Repeat the activity to have children echo your words and actions again as you name an obstacle and give notice to be cautious, such as, "There's a hole in the road. Walk cautiously!" Repeat the activity for other obstacles, stopping and raising your hand. Invite children to take turns leading.

Hands-On: Warning Folks to Be Cautious

Talk about how colored strips often alert people to be cautious in an area. Provide 3-inch-by-18-inch manila paper strips. Help children fold each strip in half lengthwise three times and then open the strip to count eight sections. Have children color the sections, alternating yellow and black, and then tape children's strips end-to-end for several long strips. Display "Be Cautious" strips appropriately, such as in block-building or paint-drying areas.

WOW! Rhyme: *cautious*

I'm a yellow traffic sign.
Here's my goal:
I am here to caution folks—
Slow! Slow! Slow!

I'm a yellow traffic light.
Here's my goal:
I say, "Please be cautious!"
Slow! Slow! Slow!

Here's What It Means

verb: to overcome something and take control

Synonyms—*They have nearly the same meaning.*

beat	succeed
defeat	win over another
overcome	achieve

Forms of *conquer* to Share with 5s

conquered (adjective, verb)

conquering (adjective, verb)

conquers (verb)

conqueror (noun)

Talk & Share

1. Wave from the top when you conquer that hill.

2. My conquered chores include setting the table.

3. The gallant knight conquered a fierce dragon.

4. My friend is conquering the rock climb.

5. The conqueror took home all the other country's gold.

6. I have conquered the challenge of tying my shoes.

7. Did you conquer the climb to the top of the pole?

8. The conquering team had the most points.

9. The wrestler in blue conquered the wrestler wearing red.

10. I want to conquer the challenge of counting to 100.

Focusing Talk: Recalling Conquered Challenges

Talk with children about the many challenges they've conquered since birth. Help children say, "I conquered it!" or "You conquered it!" while taking turns telling about conquered challenges, such as the skills of sitting up, walking, talking, growing out of car seats, or dressing themselves. You might draw a triangle to depict a mountain and write each idea up the side of the mountain. The peak might read, "Going to school."

Hands-On: Conquering New Challenges

Invite children to write or draw about two goals they'd like to conquer during an appropriate time period such as a week, month, or by the end of the school year. A goal might be learning to read or write a particular word, counting to a certain number, or reciting a poem. Children might draw or place a sticky star on each task they conquer. On the back side, children might depict how they plan to use each new skill.

WOW! Rhyme: **conquer**

Long, long ago
and in fairy-tale land,
Kings conquered kings
  and castles so grand.
And kings conquered dragons!
And kings conquered crooks!
While a king might today
  conquer reading lots of books!

Here's What It Means

verb: to save something from being used up

Synonyms—*They have nearly the same meaning.*

keep save
maintain spare
preserve

Figuratively Speaking

pinch pennies

Forms of *conserve* to Share with 5s

conservation (noun)
conserved (verb)
conserves (verb)
conserving (verb)

Talk & Share

1. We conserve electricity by turning off lights.
2. Dad asked us to take shorter showers to conserve water.
3. My conservation project is recycling aluminum cans.
4. Rainforest conservation protects the habitats of many animals.
5. Dad says we need to be conserving our money right now.
6. I conserved my sandwich at lunch, so I could eat it later.
7. Capping a marker conserves it for later use.
8. We conserve stubs of soap and then press them into a soap ball.
9. Tree conservation helps to keep our air clean.
10. I need to conserve money so I can go to college.

Focusing Talk:
Conserving Resources

Help children think about ways we use trees, one of our natural resources. On chart paper, write "Trees" above columns titled "Ways We Use" and "Ways to Conserve." Help children list uses, such as paper, furniture, house construction, ladders, doors, windows, and so on. Then list ways to conserve this resource. Ideas might include using both sides of paper, using newspaper to wrap gifts, or recycling paper.

Hands-On:
Making Reminders to Conserve Energy

Provide each child an 8-inch yarn strip, glue, and seeds or punched-out paper circles, and a colored 4-inch-by-6-inch index card that reads "Turn Off." Help children punch one hole in each top corner and then glue seeds or dry pasta to trace or outline each letter on their signs. Have children wait for glue to dry before looping the yarn through the holes and knotting each end. Children can hang their conservation signs near various on/off switches.

WOW! Rhyme: **conserve**

Earth's giving us oodles of cues
To conserve, recycle, reuse.
It's time to observe
Our need to conserve
Or lose our freedom to choose.

Here's What It Means

verb: to eat, drink, use up, or destroy something

Synonyms—*They have nearly the same meaning.*

be filled with	eat
devour	swallow
drink	use

Forms of *consume* to Share with 5s

consumed (verb)

consumer (noun)

consumes (verb)

consuming (verb)

Talk & Share

1. Billy consumed all of my jellybeans.

2. Take this vitamin after you consume your lunch.

3. My dog sneaks in and consumes the cat's food.

4. When I buy something, I am a consumer.

5. Mom said she felt consumed with the pain from her swollen ankle.

6. Hansel and Gretel consumed parts of a candy house.

7. Have all the snacks been consumed?

8. The news showed how a fire consumed the forest.

9. On Saturday, our time was consumed with yard work.

10. I feel consumed by hunger right now.

Focusing Talk: Consuming Energy

Explain or review some energy sources, such as the sun, wind, oil, coal, or gas. Talk about how plants and animals consume energy from energy sources to gain new energy to move, to breathe, or to produce other products. Read aloud "Sputter, Sputter, Sput!" (see Resources, page 181) or sing "Food Chain" (page 174). Help children identify each story's ideas about energy sources and name the energy consumers in each story.

Hands-On: Depicting a Consumer's Food Chain

Provide for each child 2-inch-by-11-inch strips of paper, one yellow (sun), one green (plant), and one red (animal). Help children write *sun, plant,* or *animal* on each strip. Have children draw a sun on its strip, loop into a circle, and glue ends together. Help children draw a plant on its strip, loop it through the yellow ring, and glue ends. Children might draw or glue a picture of a plant-eating animal on its strip and add to food chains for display.

WOW! Rhyme: *consume*

Cars consume their gasoline,

while folks consume their food.

Yes, cars and folks

are consumers alike,

BUT

Folks like their food chewed!

Here's What It Means

adjective: heavy or difficult to move

Synonyms—*They have nearly the same meaning.*

awkward   uncomfortable
bulky   unmanageable
heavy

Forms of *cumbersome* to Share with 5s

cumbersomely (adverb)
encumber (verb)
encumbered (adjective, verb)
encumbering (adjective, verb)
encumbers (verb)

Talk & Share

1. The baby's doll seems cumbersome to carry around all day.

2. An elephant moves around rather cumbersomely.

3. Backpacks with wheels are less cumbersome than the shoulder type.

4. It is cumbersome to carry this stack of library books.

5. My great-grandma can walk, but she does so cumbersomely.

6. My winter coat encumbers me such that I can barely bend my arms.

7. The furniture is cumbersome to move around the room.

8. Dad was encumbered by all his heavy packages.

9. It will be easier to use a wagon to move the cumbersome items.

10. All of those confusing ideas are encumbering my brain!

Focusing Talk:
Sorting for Cumbersome Ideas

Provide pictures of large and small, living and non-living objects or ideas. Display cards that read, "Cumbersome" and "Not Cumbersome." Scramble pictures facedown. Invite each child to pick a picture, move toward the appropriately labeled card, and report aloud, "It would feel (cumbersome/not cumbersome) to carry a (name of pictured object)." At another time, repeat to create a bulletin board display or to make a book.

Hands-On:
Relay-racing a Cumbersome Load

Conduct a relay race with a pillowcase bag filled with soft objects, such as towels, coats, small pillows, playground balls, and so on. Close it tightly with a rubber band. Position two groups in lines some 20 feet apart. Ask the first child in one line to carry the cumbersome bag to the first child in the other line, and go to the end of the line. The receiver carries the case back across the distance to a teammate. Continue until all have participated.

WOW! Rhyme: *cumbersome*

Well, the Heave-Ho Movers
are the folks you'll call to come
if your things are light as feathers,
or your load is cumbersome.
Yeah, the Heave-Ho Movers
are the folks you might encumber.
All you'll need is lots o' dollars
and the Heave-Ho Movers' number.

discourage (dis KUR ij)

Here's What It Means

verb: persuade not to do something

Synonyms—*They have nearly the same meaning.*

make unable
take hope away
try to prevent

Forms of *discourage* to Share with 5s

discouraged (verb, adjective)
discourages (verb)
discouragement (noun)
discouraging (verb, adjective)

Talk & Share

1. I felt discouraged when nobody chose me as a partner.

2. It's discouraging when someone says I can't do something.

3. I didn't want you to get into trouble, so I tried discouraging you.

4. Mom heard me sigh and understood my discouragement.

5. I felt sad when I heard those discouraging words.

6. Rainy days discourage me from going outside.

7. When you say I can't go, I feel discouraged.

8. I discouraged my dog from digging holes in the yard.

9. If no one discourages me, I might share how I'm feeling.

10. Its bad smell discouraged me from drinking the milk.

Focusing Talk:
Identifying Discouraging Words

Write the heading *Discouraging Words.* Then help children list words and phrases that can feel discouraging to hear. Examples might include *No; Go away; You can't play with us; You can't come to my birthday;* or *We don't like you.* Invite discussion about how it feels to say each word or phrase and then how it feels to hear each word or phrase. Then help children list some encouraging, or opposite, words beside each word or phrase.

Hands-On:
Sorting Discouraging and Encouraging Ideas

Invite children to observe and comment as you write on cardstock their ideas from the above activity. Cut apart the strips and help children add cut-out pictures, stickers, symbols, or drawings to illustrate each word or phrase. Invite children to match each discouraging idea with its opposite encouraging idea. Have partners rehearse dramatizations of the opposite ideas and then share in a community circle.

WOW! Rhyme: *discourage*

Don't tell me I can't do it.
Don't say I don't know how.
Please do not say discouraging words.
I need your encouragement now!

Here's What It Means

verb: to take your attention away

Synonyms—*They have nearly the same meaning.*

disturb
draw away
interrupt

Figuratively Speaking

throw a curve

Forms of *distract* to Share with 5s

distracted (verb, adjective)
distracting (verb, adjective)
distraction (noun)
distracts (verb)

Talk & Share

1. Nothing distracts me when I am reading a good book.

2. My cousin says she is easily distracted.

3. Bright headlights can distract a driver.

4. The baby's crying was distracting in the night.

5. It's hard to ignore the distraction of a ringing phone.

6. Finger tapping distracts my attention from my work.

7. I was watching my favorite show when lightning distracted me.

8. We must not distract Dad while he is driving.

9. The noise from the playroom distracted my mom as she worked.

10. A runaway dog caused a distraction outside my classroom.

Focusing Talk: Considering Distractions

Help children create a "Distractions" T-chart to list ideas of possible distractions, such as a TV, someone talking, a clock's ticking, or water dripping. Help children list distracting ideas down the left side of the chart, and on the right side list at least one way to cope with or avoid each distraction. Talk about how people feel differently about distracting ideas. Discuss how coping ideas may work for some folks, but not for others.

Hands-On: Trying to Distract

Invite partners to practice this activity before sharing with the group. Have partners take turns trying to focus on an activity, such as reading or pretending to watch a soccer game, as the other child works to create a distraction to draw attention away from the book or game. Help children make thoughtful choices as they rehearse so that everyone feels comfortable physically and emotionally. Compare and contrast the distracting ideas.

WOW! Rhyme: **distract**

My dog was distracting
when I was subtracting.
Her licking distracted—
and I lost my place.

I allowed her distraction
to stop my subtraction.
But I like this distraction—
she's licking my face!

Here's What It Means
adjective: excited or very interested

Synonyms—*They have nearly the same meaning.*
eager
happily
looking forward to

Figuratively Speaking
tickled pink; ball of fire; fired up; full of energy; pumped; ready to roll; filled with gusto

Forms of *enthusiastic* to Share with 5s
enthused (adjective)
enthusiasm (noun)
enthusiast (noun)
enthusiastically (adverb)

Talk & Share
1. My sister talked enthusiastically about going to the carnival.
2. Listen to the enthusiasm of those fans!
3. Billy is not enthused about going to the dentist.
4. I am a tropical fish enthusiast.
5. The children ran out enthusiastically at recess time.
6. Dad is enthusiastic about baseball and watches all the games.
7. Her eyes sparkled with enthusiasm when she saw her cousins.
8. Annie enthusiastically tore open her gift.
9. My papa's a book enthusiast.
10. I packed quickly because I felt enthusiastic about the sleepover.

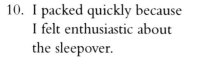

Focusing Talk:
Identifying Enthusiastic Behaviors
Using the word *enthusiastic* in a sentence, tell children about an expression or action you witnessed and what you think may have caused that enthusiasm. Set a timer for 2 minutes and invite partners to use facial expressions or actions (giggling, huge smile, clapping, shout-outs, etc.) to show enthusiasm. Ask children to use the WOW! Word and its forms in sentences to tell about enthusiastic behaviors they saw or heard.

Hands-On:
Supporting with Enthusiasm
Display a pennant (elongated triangle sometimes attached to a stick for waving), and tell children that people often display pennants to show enthusiasm for a favorite high school or college team. Provide pennant-shaped triangles cut from 11-inch-by-14-inch paper. Help children use words and pictures to make pennants to show enthusiastic support for a favorite team, school, or activity. Have children check at home for pennants owned by family members.

WOW! Rhyme: *enthusiastic*
I feel enthusiastic! Rah-rah-rah!
I feel enthusiastic! Sis-boom-bah!
I love to sing and play!
I get to sing today!
I feel enthusiastic! Rah-rah-rah!
I feel enthusiastic! Sis-boom-bah!

Note: Repeat the WOW! Rhyme to substitute other verbs for *sing* in lines three and four, such as *dance, read, draw, paint, build, run, lead, write, jump, sleep, race, eat,* or *hug.*

Here's What It Means

noun: a mistake

Synonyms—*They have nearly the same meaning.*

accident   flaw

blunder   mishap

Figuratively Speaking

bad move; boo-boo; botch it up; goof; uh-oh

Forms of *error* to Share with 5s

err (verb)

erred (verb)

erroneous (adjective)

errors (noun)

Talk & Share

1. Mom made an error when she wrote a check.

2. There's an error on the menu.

3. I found two errors on my paper.

4. I gave you the toy in error because it was not mine.

5. We made an error and bought the wrong soap.

6. Oops, I erred when I said that.

7. The first school supply list included some errors.

8. My thinking was erroneous just now.

9. I'll try not to err.

10. I erased all the errors on my paper.

Focusing Talk: Making Errors

Invite groups of three to think of collections of three sentences in which one sentence has no relationship to the other two. Give an example, such as *I played ball. I swam. Mom is here.* Help children recognize that two sentences tell about a sport, while the third does not. Invite groups to share their sentences in a community circle for classmates to identify the sentence that is in error or does not belong with the others. Have children tell why.

Hands-On: Spotting Errors

Prepare several sets such that one item does not belong in each. Examples may include: yellow square in set of yellow circles; yellow circle in set of yellow squares; an animal picture in a set of vehicle pictures; letter M with set of numbers. You may want to introduce the word *anomaly* to describe what doesn't belong in each set. Invite children to use *error* and *anomaly* in sentences to talk about why each item doesn't belong.

WOW! Rhyme: **error**

I made an error.

I erred.

I did.

So I used my eraser.

And my error?

It hid!

flexible (FLEK suh buhl)

Here's What It Means

adjective: able to be moved

Synonyms—*They have nearly the same meaning.*

agreeable   open to
bendable   willing
moveable

Figuratively Speaking

loose; open to change

Forms of *flexible* to Share with 5s

flex (verb)
flexibility (noun)
inflexible (adjective)

Talk & Share

1. My skin is flexible.

2. Aunt Sky says arthritis makes her joints inflexible.

3. Mom thinks her calendar is flexible next week.

4. This bandage is so flexible that it's still on my knuckle.

5. I like straws that are flexible.

6. I fell and quickly remembered how inflexible a sidewalk is!

7. We make our own flexible dough to play with and make things.

8. The waistband on these shorts is flexible.

9. There's a limit to the flexibility of a rubber band.

10. Watch me flex my muscles!

Focusing Talk: Using Flexibility

Have children follow your lead as you read and act out "Bend and Stretch" (see Resources, page 175). Discuss how muscles give people and animals flexibility to move about. Invite children to chant the poem and end with a whisper-chant, "I am flexible! I can bend and stretch!" Whisper-chanting is effective as a behavior-management tool. You might use a flexible toy skeleton as you read and sing "My Bones" (see Resources, page 179).

Hands-On: Flexing Flexible Creatures

Provide play dough for children to create flexible creatures. Have children name and share their creations with the group, telling how each creature's flexibility allows it to move this way or that. You may also invite children to move their creatures, or bring in flexible rubber toys, flexing their flexible creatures accordingly as you read the poem "Bend and Stretch" (see Resources, page 175) or the WOW! Rhyme below.

WOW! Rhyme: **flexible**

I am fairly flexible.
Watch how I can bend.
I have flexibility.
I bend from end to end!

Here's What It Means

adjective: out of control because of worry or fear

Synonyms—*They have nearly the same meaning.*

desperate   overly excited

distressed   panicky

Figuratively Speaking

at the end of my rope; at wit's end; climbing the wall

Form of *frantic* to Share with 5s

frantically (adverb)

Talk & Share

1. My dog often acts frantically during a storm.

2. My brother searched frantically for the missing house key.

3. The frantic look on her face caused others to worry.

4. The lady ran frantically to catch the bus before it left the bus stop.

5. Mom packed frantically so she could catch her flight.

6. He was so frantic about finishing on time that he forgot to sign his name.

7. When I saw the accident, I ran frantically for help.

8. The last runner on the relay team grabbed frantically at the baton.

9. I can solve a problem better when I'm not feeling so frantic.

10. When Shaighla feels frantic, she simply counts slowly to ten.

Focusing Talk:
Talking about Frantic Feelings

Create an "Everyone Has Frantic Feelings" T-chart with column heads, "I felt frantic when…" and "Next time I might.…" Share an experience, such as "I felt frantic when my cat got out." Write children's ideas (feeling lost, going to doctor, being late, etc.). Help children add ideas for ways to feel less frantic in each situation. Discuss how everyone experiences feeling frantic and how helpful it can be to talk about ways to cope.

Hands-On:
Dramatizing Frantic Feelings and Giving Empathy

Read aloud "My Faces" (see Resources, page 179). Have partners take turns telling about a situation that caused them to feel frantic. As one talks, help listening partners show silently the range of facial expressions, such as worry to fear to relief to happiness, one might wear when having such an experience. Repeat for partners to take turns wearing the feelings faces or watching to name a feeling behind each feeling face.

WOW! Rhyme: *frantic*

I was feeling frantic.

Really frantic—full of fear.

Until I told my frantic self,

"Fears, go disappear!"

Here's What It Means

adverb: often

Synonyms—They have nearly the same meaning.

a number of times	happens a lot
again and again	often but not always
almost all the time	over and over

Forms of *frequently* to Share with 5s

frequent (adjective)

frequency (noun)

Talk & Share

1. I frequently ask questions.

2. People frequently go to birthday parties.

3. I go to the movies frequently.

4. Grandma visits us frequently.

5. Who likes frequent trips to the zoo?

6. My dog barks frequently at sounds in the house.

7. Does it snow frequently in the mountains?

8. The weather here is frequently sunny.

9. Frequent use of the map kept me from getting lost.

10. It's important to wash my hands frequently.

Focusing Talk: Noting Frequent Activities

Tell about an activity, such as gardening or checking e-mail, that you do frequently but not all the time. Model use of quotation marks as you record children's sentences about activities they do often but not always: *[child's name] said, "I often play outside but not always. That means I frequently play outside."* List more examples, such as *sleep, play, work, talk, listen, eat, read,* and *walk.* This activity also helps to develop a test-taking skill.

Hands-On: Recording Frequent Sightings

Invite children to cut out pictures of items frequently found in a house but not in every house. Children might also identify pictures of items frequently found, but not always, in other places or locations, such as in a vehicle, kitchen, bedroom, bathroom, grocery store, zoo, school, office, yard, or street. Invite children to choose a location and glue appropriate pictures on a sheet of paper, add a title, and share ideas with family members.

WOW! Rhyme: *frequently*

I frequently work.

And I frequently play.

So I'm frequently tired

at the end of the day!

Here's What It Means

verb: to pay no attention to

Synonyms—*They have nearly the same meaning.*

disregard

not notice

shut out

Forms of *ignore* to Share with 5s

ignored (verb, adjective)

ignores (verb)

ignoring (verb, adjective)

Talk & Share

1. I had to ignore outside noises so I could do my work.

2. I ignored those mean words.

3. It's hard to ignore rude behavior.

4. Mom seemed to ignore what I'd said.

5. I hope you won't ignore my opinion.

6. Will you please ignore what I said yesterday?

7. Ignoring her noises might help me pay attention.

8. My cat will not allow me to ignore her.

9. She ignores the phone when she needs to get something done.

10. I had to ignore the bright light so I could get to sleep.

Focusing Talk: Ignoring Annoyances

Tell children about a time you worked hard to ignore something, such as a noise while trying to work; words that felt unkind and mean-spirited; bothersome behavior; or a leaky faucet. Help children use *ignore* and its forms as they tell about times when they have felt annoyed and knew they needed to ignore something. Talk about how the words *ignore* and *annoy* sound somewhat alike because they each include the medial sound of /n/.

Hands-On: Helping Others Ignore Things

Provide copied pictures of various characters, along with markers and small, plain stickers. Invite children to use stickers or markers to give each character earmuffs, earplugs, nose covers, or blinders to indicate ways to ignore a loud noise or unpleasant sight, smell, or taste. Encourage children to try moving or rotating a character away from an annoyance. Help children share and tell about their ideas in a community circle.

> WOW! Rhyme: **ignore**
>
> I'll try to ignore it.
> I'll try not to hear.
> I'm gonna imagine—
>   kind words in my ear.

Here's What It Means

adjective: to feel bothered or annoyed
verb: to have bothered or annoyed

Synonyms—*They have nearly the same meaning.*

cranky   sore
cross   touchy
grouchy   troubled
grumpy   upset

Figuratively Speaking

going bananas; feeling ticked off;
not a happy camper

Forms of *irritated* to Share with 5s

irritable (adjective)
irritate (verb)
irritates (verb)
irritating (verb, adjective)
irritation (noun)

Talk & Share

1. I feel irritated when someone pushes in line.

2. Mom grew irritable when the phone kept ringing.

3. I find myself getting irritated easily today.

4. My shoe keeps irritating my sore toe.

5. Our baby gets irritated and cries if we don't pick him up.

6. Some say e-mails can be an irritation, but they like it anyway.

7. Bad manners irritate my parents.

8. That sound is irritating when I'm trying to read.

9. My wet swimsuit irritates my skin.

10. I feel irritated when my friend won't talk to me.

Focusing Talk:
Telling About Needs and Irritations

Model statements, such as "I feel irritated right now because I need…" or "When I needed to sleep, I felt irritated." Then help children follow your models to describe situations when they have felt irritated. Encourage each statement to include the need that brought about the feeling of irritation. Other examples might include a need to have no noise or a need for quiet, a need to make a zipper work, a need to find something; and so on.

Hands-On:
Identifying Expressions of Irritation

Read aloud "My Faces" (see Resources, page 179). Provide scissors and old magazines. Help children identify and cut out pictures of faces that show irritation and faces that show little or no irritation. Encourage use of *irritated* and its forms as children share their pictures in a community circle. Children might sort pictures for opposite and similar feelings, or by similarly aged persons. Help children create their own book about faces.

WOW! Rhyme: **irritated**

It's irritating—this tag on my shirt.
It's irritating my skin.
I turned it around,
but now that tag
is irritating my chin!

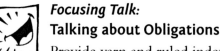

Here's What It Means

noun: something that you need to do

Synonyms—*They have nearly the same meaning.*

agreement	promise
burden	requirement
commitment	responsibility
duty	

Form of *obligation* to Share with 5s

obligated (adjective)

Talk & Share

1. I have an obligation to feed my pet.

2. Classmates are obligated to help each other keep the room clean.

3. I am being responsible when I take care of my obligations.

4. My dad forgot to get milk, so he felt obligated to go back to the store.

5. Do you feel obligated to recycle to help the environment?

6. Melanie ought to feel obligated to share her cookie with me.

7. Max felt obligated to let Kimba get back in line.

8. Some days I am obligated to walk my brother to school.

9. My obligations are to push in the chairs and wipe off the table.

10. Our teacher asked if we felt obligated to shake hands.

Focusing Talk:
Talking about Obligations

Provide yarn and ruled index cards for children to create "My Obligations" signage to illustrate daily obligations at home. While working with partners, encourage children to tell one another details about each daily obligation, their feelings about the chore, and how meeting an obligation to complete a task helps their entire family. Help children punch holes to attach yarn for hanging their signs, perhaps on bedroom doorknobs.

Hands-On:
Showing Obligations on a Bar Graph

Create a large vertical bar graph on chart paper. Starting 1 inch or so above the bottom, draw a line—the X axis—across from left to right. Similarly, draw the Y axis 1 inch in and up the left side. Write children's obligations, such as "make bed," "feed pet," "brush teeth," and so on, about 4 inches apart along the X axis. Write "Number of Children" up the Y axis. Help children write their initials on sticky notes and attach one note for each obligation.

WOW! Rhyme: **obligation**

I feel an obligation
to be helpful to my friend.
And I'll meet my obligation
from beginning to the end.

Here's What It Means

verb: to look very carefully or to notice something

Synonyms—*They have nearly the same meaning.*

examine	spot
inspect	study
notice	watch
respect	witness
see	

Forms of *observe* to Share with 5s

observant (adjective)

observation (noun)

observatory (noun)

observed (verb)

observer (noun)

observes (verb)

observing (verb)

Talk & Share

1. Observe the dance so you can learn it, too.

2. We observed the turtle eating mustard greens.

3. We used binoculars to observe the baby birds in their nest.

4. They use an observation tower to check for forest fires.

5. We identified the planets from an observatory deck.

6. Our observant dog notices any hole in the fence.

7. Drivers must observe traffic laws.

8. Mayla observes all the holidays with her family.

9. We have been observing how a caterpillar changes to a butterfly.

10. Our newspaper is called *The Community Observer*.

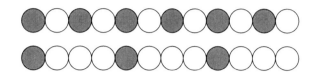

Focusing Talk: Observing and Creating Patterns

Share "My True Story" (see Resources, page 179) and help children observe and tell about the poem's pattern. Explain that some patterns are simple, while other patterns may be more complicated. Demonstrate a row of colored blocks or crayons in a pattern, such as red/blue/blue/red/blue/blue and so on. Help children use sentences to tell what they observe. Have partners take turns to create a pattern, observe, name the pattern, and duplicate it.

Hands-On: Preserving Observed Patterns

Provide lightweight paper and crayons for making rubbings of patterns children observe inside and outside. You may want to model how to expose the veins of a leaf by placing the leaf between lightweight papers and rubbing the side of a crayon across the top paper. Help children make leaf rubbings and rubbings of other patterns, such as a tree's bark, a cut tree's cross-section, a pattern on a rock, a slab of concrete, textured surfaces, and so on.

WOW! Rhyme: *observe*

He observed it all,

or so he's said.

He's said he observed

how she hit her head.

His observation

of the clown's falling down

is an observation

not shared by the clown!

Here's What It Means

adjective: once in a while

Synonyms—*They have nearly the same meaning.*

infrequent	odd
not happening often	rare
not regularly	uncommon
now and then	

Figuratively Speaking

from time to time; a sometimes thing; once in a blue moon

Forms of *occasional* to Share with 5s

occasion (noun)
occasionally (adverb)

Talk & Share

1. Dad and I take occasional walks around our neighborhood.

2. Before a special occasion, I occasionally take a nap.

3. Our block tower occasionally falls down.

4. It's an occasion when Mom lets us stay up until midnight.

5. My big sister likes an occasional hug.

6. My best friend and I argue occasionally.

7. On occasion, Grandma says that we can have a piece of candy.

8. Ricardo occasionally pushes me on the swing.

9. Though Sam's a good reader, he occasionally needs help with a word.

10. Our class enjoys our principal's occasional visits.

Focusing Talk:
Comparing Occasional Occurrences

Help children create a human bar graph to compare enjoyment of an occasional event, such as eating pizza on Monday or going to the zoo. Invite children to use *occasional* or a form in a sentence to say, "I occasionally go to the zoo" and stand to form a line. Ask children who do not have that occasional experience to line up parallel to the first line. Help compare the lines to tell if more or fewer children enjoy the event occasionally.

Hands-On:
Remembering Occasional Experiences

Provide five index cards and a clothes hanger for each child. Ask children to illustrate five different joyful experiences they have occasionally. Some may want to draw the same thing on both sides of a card. Have children use yarn or string cut in random lengths to hang the five cards from a coat hanger. Help children display their mobiles so that, while resting, they can observe and think about occasional experiences that are joyful.

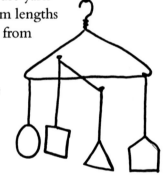

WOW! Rhyme: **occasional**

Occasionally, I help my Gram.
Occasionally, Gram and I play.
And sometimes, my grandmother says to me,
"An occasional nap's okay!"

Here's What It Means

adjective: the first one like it

Synonyms—*They have nearly the same meaning.*

beginning	imaginative
clever	new
creative	starting
very different	unusual

Figuratively Speaking

one of a kind; outside the box; unlike anything else

Forms of *original* to Share with 5s

origin (noun)
originality (noun)
originally (adverb)
originate (verb)
originator (noun)

Talk & Share

1. Please line up in your original order.

2. He originally took out the blocks.

3. We changed the original plan.

4. No one knows the origin of this plant.

5. Your hairstyle shows a lot of originality!

6. Annie originally blamed John until she heard all the facts.

7. I see the originality in your unusual artwork.

8. Did the secret originate with you?

9. Your choice shows original thinking.

10. Who was the originator of that toy?

Focusing Talk: Telling an Original Story

Read aloud a story, such as *Corduroy* (see Resources, page 173). Hold a stuffed animal and begin to tell a story that includes a name for the animal; a setting, such as a library; and a problem, such as the animal's being hungry. Invite each child to add a sentence to the story to add one original detail. You may want to write or record the story as it's told. Write initials or say "by [child's name]" to indicate each child's original thinking.

Hands-On: Playing an Original Circle Game

Tell children that long ago—or even now in some communities—some people called a girl a *lassie* and a boy a *laddie*. Invite children to stand in a circle. Have one child step into the center and make up an original dance movement while others imitate the movement and use *lassie* or *laddie* to chant or sing, "Did You Ever See a Lassie?" (see Resources, page 177). Take turns for others to play the role of the originator who leads the group.

WOW! Rhyme: *original*

They're different!
Creative!
They're wacky!
They're new!
I like those original things that you do.

Here's What It Means

verb: to get someone to do something

Synonyms—*They have nearly the same meaning.*

win over
make someone believe
convince

Figuratively Speaking

sell an idea

Forms of *persuade* to Share with 5s

persuaded (verb)
persuades (verb)
persuading (verb)
persuasion (noun)

Talk & Share

1. I tried to persuade her to go with us.

2. Grandpa was persuaded to try my new recipe.

3. I can't persuade him to tell his secret.

4. Don't try to persuade me to do that.

5. I think I'll try persuading Dad to take me fishing.

6. Sunshine persuades me to go outside.

7. My dog persuaded me to take him for a walk.

8. I will try to persuade my friends to talk quietly.

9. If we get a computer, I might be persuaded to write more stories.

10. With some persuasion, I might learn to like beets.

Focusing Talk: Finding Persuasive Pictures

Invite children to observe how persuasive pictures can be. Present two books such that one has a colorful, enticing cover while the other has less colorful and interesting art. Help children use *persuade* and its forms to tell why one book's cover might persuade them to want to take a closer look. Have children look inside the books to tell which pictures might help persuade readers to read on. Repeat to compare more pairs of books.

Hands-On: Exploring Persuasive Advertising

Provide old magazines and newspapers. Invite children to cut out pictured advertisements that persuade them to want to know more about the advertised item. Once children have identified two or three ads, invite partners to share their finds and tell each other why they think each ad is persuasive. At another time, help children similarly explore product packaging or report on how certain products are placed in stores to attract children.

> *WOW!* Rhyme: **persuade**
>
> Persuade me to do it.
> Convince me I should.
> Though persuasion won't work
> if ideas aren't good.

Here's What It Means

verb: to not allow

Synonyms—*They have nearly the same meaning.*

ban	outlaw
forbid	prevent
halt	restrict
not permit	stop

Figuratively Speaking

a no-no; uh-uh

Forms of *prohibit* to Share with 5s

prohibited (adjective, verb)

prohibiting (verb)

prohibits (verb)

Talk & Share

1. School rules prohibit chewing gum.

2. Smoking is prohibited in most places.

3. My heavy coat is prohibiting me from raising my arms.

4. A "No Trespassing" sign might help to prohibit unwanted visitors.

5. Mom prohibited playing until Dee's homework was done.

6. A broken leg prohibited Dustin from playing in the soccer game.

7. The crossing guard is there to prohibit cars as we cross the street.

8. Bullying is prohibited at my school.

9. Our new rule prohibits my sister from calling me names.

10. We're prohibited from getting new library books until we return our other books.

Focusing Talk:
Listing Rules That Prohibit Behaviors

Invite children to share rules that guide behaviors at school, home, or in other places. Help children use *prohibit* and its forms to share each rule. For example, "No running in the halls" might be stated, "Running in the halls is prohibited." Write each rule on a sentence strip. Help children sort the sentences according to where each rule applies. For example, sentences might list classroom rules, home rules, bus rules, or car rules.

Hands-On:
Making Signs to Prohibit Behaviors

Share a universal symbol that is meant to prohibit a behavior. For example, prohibited parking may be signaled by a circle showing a car or large "P" with a line drawn diagonally over it. Provide pre-cut circles. Invite children to reference their rules above and draw or glue pictures to make signs. Show children how to drag the side of a crayon to make a thick line around the edge of a circle and to draw a diagonal across the circle.

WOW! Rhyme: *prohibit*

Talking is prohibited,

though we all like to talk.

Running is prohibited,

though we don't want to walk.

Eating is prohibited,

though we are eating treats.

Lots of things prohibited—

so we don't want those seats!

Here's What It Means

adjective: like the real thing

Synonyms—*They have nearly the same meaning.*

actual	good
accurate	natural
exact	pure
existing	serious
genuine	true

Figuratively Speaking

dose of reality; getting real; reality check

Forms of *realistic* to Share with 5s

realism (noun)
realistically (adverb)
reality (noun)

Talk & Share

1. Your drawing of a dog looks realistic.

2. I have to be realistic about how much money to spend.

3. In reality, we've run out of time.

4. The realism of the actor's performance made me believe he died.

5. I can realistically hop thirty times in a row.

6. The realism of that fake flower fooled the bees.

7. It is still raining and, realistically speaking, it could flood.

8. I don't like to watch reality television shows.

9. Please be realistic when you tell me what you want.

10. The reality is that I must practice more.

Focusing Talk:
Speaking Realistically

Read poems that present realistic and unrealistic themes, such as those by Hajdusiewicz, Hopkins, Prelutsky, or Silverstein (see Resources, page 174). Help children use the word *realistic* and its forms as they discuss each poem. You might also share "My True Story" (see Resources, page 179) and "Fiction" (page 177) for children to be judges who give a "thumbs up" for a *realistic* idea they hear or a "thumbs down" for an *unrealistic* idea.

Hands-On:
Exploring Realistic Details

Provide old magazines for children to cut out realistic pictures of animals. Have children fold drawing paper in half, open, and glue an animal's picture onto the left side. Discuss each animal's features and such details that could help to make a sketch of that animal look realistic. Then invite children to draw their animals as realistically as they can on the right side of the fold. Have children write their initials on their work and share at home.

> *WOW!* Rhyme: **realistic**
>
> I could rule the galaxy!
> Oops, here's what I meant...
> I could, realistically,
> become our president.

Here's What It Means

verb: to suggest

Synonyms—*They have nearly the same meaning.*

advise   suggest
encourage   support
praise

Forms of *recommend* to Share with 5s

recommendation (noun)
recommended (verb)
recommending (verb)
recommends (verb)

Talk & Share

1. Do you recommend that we play kickball during recess?

2. My teacher recommends that I play every day to become a better player.

3. The vet recommends a daily walk for our dog.

4. Three of my friends gave the new movie good recommendations.

5. The note recommended digging for buried treasure under the tree.

6. I recommend that you tie your shoes before you run the race.

7. When I couldn't decide, my sister recommended choosing the blue one.

8. Mr. Marshall wrote a letter of recommendation to help Sarah get a job.

9. I'm recommending that you spend your free time in the block center.

10. I recommend eating the peaches before they are too ripe.

Focusing Talk: Recommending a Book

Invite children to think of a favorite book they would like to recommend that others might read. Encourage use of the words *I recommend* as children give a reason to support their recommendation and then follow up that reason with a detail from the book that supports the reason. As children make such recommendations or claims, followed by support or elaboration, they are learning a useful pattern for later writing of book reviews.

Hands-On: Recommending Activity Centers

Provide index cards and glue, along with a disposable or digital camera. Help partners take turns photographing one another while involved in an activity center each child might recommend to others. Have children mount photos on index cards and add a word or phrase that identifies the recommended activity. They can then hole-punch the corner of each card to attach to large binder rings for hanging near the recommended center.

WOW! Rhyme: *recommend*

I recommend you just eat two.
I recommend you draw with blue.
I recommend you use the glue.
I recommend you tie your shoe.
I recommend…
you ought to do
the things that I'm
recommending to you.

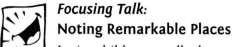

WOW! Word **remarkable** (ri MAR kuh buhl)

Here's What It Means

adjective: extra special

Synonyms—*They have nearly the same meaning.*

extraordinary   surprising
outstanding   uncommon
rare   unusual
striking

Figuratively Speaking

stands out from the rest; awesome

Form of *remarkable* to Share with 5s

remarkably (adverb)

Talk & Share

1. I saw a remarkable light in the sky.
2. My neighbor says my manners are remarkable.
3. Uncle Ike was a remarkable chess player when he was in college.
4. The weather today has been remarkably warm.
5. Who made this remarkable drawing?
6. Dad read a remarkable book to me.
7. She skates remarkably well for a beginner.
8. I think mangoes have a remarkable taste.
9. It was remarkable when our baby stood all by herself.
10. He took remarkable photographs of the ice storm.

Focusing Talk: Noting Remarkable Places

Invite children to talk about remarkable places they have visited and tell why each locale felt special to them. Help children recognize that the idea of being remarkable is an opinion and, therefore, varies from person to person. Talk about routine or ordinary places children visit—such as the grocery store, the kitchen, or a relative's home—that may seem remarkable on a particular day, such as right after the refrigerator has been restocked.

Hands-On: Using My Remarkable Senses

Help children cut out pictures from old magazines to create a collection titled "My Remarkable Nose Can Smell!" Pictures might include a nose that's sniffing foods cooking, baby powder, and smoke from a fire. "My Remarkable Eyes Can See!" might depict eyes watching children at play, a river, and blossoms on a tree. A book titled "My Remarkable Senses" could serve to help children review all five senses.

WOW! Rhyme: **remarkable**

Each remarkable sound
and remarkable sight
made the Fourth of July
a remarkable night!

From *WOW! Words* Copyright ©2011 Babs Bell Hajdusiewicz. This page may be reproduced for classroom use only. www.goodyearbooks.com.

resemble (ri ZEM buhl)

Here's What It Means

verb: to appear like something else

Synonyms—*They have nearly the same meaning.*

looks like   is similar to
takes after   is the same as
matches   compares to
mirrors

Forms of *resemble* to Share with 5s

resemblance (noun)
resembled (verb)
resembles (verb)

Talk & Share

1. My nose resembles my dad's nose.
2. That cloud resembles a rabbit.
3. That hat resembles the one Abraham Lincoln wore.
4. As babies, my brother and I had a strong resemblance to each other.
5. Jocelynn made a sand sculpture that resembles a crocodile.
6. The scarecrow resembled an old man.
7. Our dog drawings resemble one another.
8. Identical twins have a really close resemblance to one another.
9. Butterflies resemble moths in many ways.
10. The tablecloth resembled a checkerboard.

Focusing Talk:
Using Resemble to Innovate on Texts

Read aloud *It Looked Like Spilt Milk.* Reread to model substituting *resembled* for the words *looked like* to say, "Sometimes it resembled a bird." Help children follow your model to assist you in rereading the book. At other times, similarly substitute *resemble* in *Little Cloud, Harold and the Purple Crayon,* or *Quick as a Cricket* (see Resources, page 173). You might also help children use *resemble* to describe an item for others to name.

Hands-On:
Playing "What Do I Resemble?"

Invite children to stand in a circle. Then form two circles by having every other child step forward and turn around to form an inner circle that faces the outer circle. Have children dance in their circles as music plays. When music stops, children in the outer circle freeze in the resemblance of something recognizable, such as a tree, dog, cat, giraffe, frog, or turtle. Inner-circle children who guess their partner's character can exchange places.

WOW! Rhyme: *resemble*

I resemble my mom.
Someone said so today.
And for that, I am glad,
but it's also okay
to resemble my gram or my sis or
   Aunt Pat.
But I wouldn't be happy resembling
   our cat.

Here's What It Means

verb: to begin again

Synonyms—*They have nearly the same meaning.*

continue   pick up

go on   start again

Figuratively Speaking

get on with it

Forms of *resume* to Share with 5s

resumed (verb)

resumes (verb)

resuming (verb)

Talk & Share

1. We'll have to resume the game another day.
2. He quickly resumed talking.
3. No one can resume traveling now that the bridge is up.
4. I get to resume swimming now that my cast is off.

5. Let's try to resume where we left off.
6. Resume whenever you are ready.
7. Please resume reading.
8. We're resuming our drive up the mountain.
9. The car can't resume without gas.
10. The play resumes in a few minutes.

Focusing Talk:
Resuming Activities Easily... or Not

Ask if it's easy to resume sleep when awakened in the night. Ask why or why not. List activities that are easy or difficult to resume once interrupted. "Easy to Resume" examples might include playing a soccer game; reading a book; peeling an orange; telling a story; climbing a ladder; or walking backward. "Difficult to Resume" examples might include baking a cake; sneezing; catching a runaway pet; or swallowing.

Hands-On:
Resuming a Popping Task

Provide one 6-inch-by-12-inch bubble packing strip for each group of four children. Tell children they are to press and pop two bubbles in order and quickly give it to the next person; the second person resumes the action by popping two bubbles in order from the first person's and passes the bubble strip to the next person, and so on until the strip is flat. Set a timer for 5 minutes. Children will enjoy this noisy challenge of resuming another's job as the sheet passes from popper to popper.

WOW! Rhyme: *resume*

Let us resume!

We get to go on.

The parade can resume

since that downpour is gone.

Here's What It Means

verb: to give the main ideas in a shortened form

Synonyms—*They have nearly the same meaning.*

main points   retelling
outline   review

Forms of *summarize* to Share with 5s

summaries (noun)
summarized (verb)
summarizes (verb)
summarizing (verb)
summary (noun)

Talk & Share

1. Please summarize what happened before the lamp fell.

2. I remember stories because I summarize them after I read them.

3. Our librarian gives us summaries of the new books she has read.

4. Mom likes to hear a summary of my day at school.

5. The movie reviewer summarizes each new movie.

6. After listening to your summary, I think you have a good plan.

7. I summarized the TV show for my sister because she had missed it.

8. Some newspapers include a summary of each longer story.

9. "Make safe choices!" could summarize our playground rules.

10. In summarizing a lesson, we name the main ideas.

Focusing Talk:
Summarizing a Story

Read aloud a folk or fairy tale, such as "The Three Bears" or "Rumpelstiltskin." Write *B—M—E* on chart paper. Remind children that a good story has a beginning, middle, and end. Using a call-and-response pattern, point to the *B* and ask, "Who will help summarize the story's beginning?" for a child to respond, "I will help summarize the beginning." Continue for *M* and *E* to complete the summary.

Hands-On:
Making and Using Book Summaries

Provide blank books made of two sheets of paper folded such that each consecutive edge extends half-an-inch beyond the previous page, forming four tabs. Help children write on their cover a favorite book's title, along with letters *B, M,* and *E* in order on the three tabs. Help children write or draw the main idea of the book's beginning, middle, and end. Display for children to review books they'd like to read or check out to share at home.

WOW! Rhyme: **summarize**

She asked what happened.
I didn't want to tell.
So I thought it wise
to summarize:
"I jumped. I bumped. It fell."

Here's What It Means

verb: to put you in danger

Synonyms—*They have nearly the same meaning.*

bully   put at risk
endanger   scare

Figuratively Speaking

read the riot act; show 'em who's boss

Forms of *threaten* to Share with 5s

threat (noun)
threatened (verb, adjective)
threatening (verb, adjective)
threatens (verb)
threats (noun)

Talk & Share

1. A big dog threatened me on my way to school.

2. I heard the girl threaten to hit other kids.

3. Smoking cigarettes threatens people's good health.

4. The sky looks like it is threatening to rain.

5. The bully's threats stopped when I spoke up for myself.

6. My mom threatened to take away all toys left on the floor.

7. My little brother laughs when I act like a threatening monster.

8. Jack's threat seemed harsh, but it helped everyone tell the truth.

9. The police officer threatened to take the thief to jail.

10. I feel threatened when I see an animal growl.

Focusing Talk:
Discussing Behaviors That Threaten

Read aloud from the following: *Little Red Riding Hood, There's a Nightmare in My Closet, Make Way for Ducklings, The Three Little Pigs,* or "Bulldog Bully" (see Resources, pages 173–176). Help children use *threaten* and its forms in sentences to tell how they think each story character might be feeling. Invite children to help list strategies or plans that characters used, or might have used, to cope with or to prevent a felt threat.

Hands-On:
Reenacting Threatening Situations

Provide folded cardstock for each child. Ask children to name a threatening situation, such as a tornado, a fire in a hallway, or clothing that's on fire. Help children write on their front cover a title, such as "Steps to Take When (named threat)" and draw pictures inside to denote the sequence of steps they might suggest to be safe in the face of that threat. Invite children to use stuffed animals to dramatize their threatening situations.

WOW! Rhyme: **threaten**

The sky suggests it's threatening to rain.

A bully suggests there's a threat of some pain.

A dog suggests it's threatening to bite.

And me?

I threaten to hug... real tight!

Here's What It Means

adjective: very large

Synonyms—*They have nearly the same meaning.*

amazing	great
awesome	marvelous
enormous	terrific
grand	wonderful

Form of *tremendous* to Share with 5s

tremendously (adverb)

Talk & Share

1. Someone did a tremendous job here!

2. My lunch is tremendous today.

3. I felt tremendously tired last night.

4. It was tremendous to see my dad arrive.

5. I received a tremendous number of cards.

6. A tremendous crowd attended the carnival.

7. With this hearing aid, I hear tremendously well.

8. I'm tremendously happy right now.

9. She should be tremendously surprised.

10. I have some tremendous news to share!

Focusing Talk:
Using My Tremendous Senses

Read "Fighting Makes No Sense!" (see Resources, page 177). Then model sharing how a sense helped you have a tremendous experience: "My tremendous ears helped me hear a tremendous song on the radio." Invite children to share similarly. You may want to similarly focus on tremendous sensory experiences via the other senses, such as eyes to read a book, tongue to taste a food, nose to smell a flower, or fingers to feel a cotton ball.

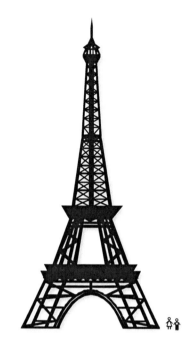

Hands-On:
Making Tremendous Creations

Invite partners to use materials, such as clay, blocks, chenille sticks, cardboard, or other recycled materials to create structures that meet certain specs. For example, a cup or can might be a model for minimum height. Talk about why *tremendous* is a judgmental word and, thus, its use will vary depending on who is judging and on that person's view and opinion of the structure's qualities, such as uniqueness, size, color, or texture.

WOW! Rhyme: **tremendous**

This playground's tremendous.
I like the tall slide.
I'm climbing!
I'm jumping!
Look here... I can hide!

undoubtedly (uhn DOW tuhd lee)

Here's What It Means

adverb: definitely true

Synonyms—*They have nearly the same meaning.*

absolutely	truly
certainly	unquestionably
positively	without a doubt
surely	

Figuratively Speaking

hands down

Forms of *undoubtedly* to Share with 5s

doubt (noun, verb)
doubtful (adjective)

Talk & Share

1. You undoubtedly have the biggest piece of pizza.

2. A 500-piece puzzle is undoubtedly a challenge.

3. Your dog undoubtedly barks the loudest in our neighborhood.

4. I doubt this will be our most severe storm this season.

5. You will undoubtedly remember when Grandma dropped the cake.

6. Some people undoubtedly select a window seat on a plane.

7. It's doubtful that she'll be the first to arrive.

8. Abby is undoubtedly the best runner in our class.

9. That is undoubtedly a drawing of a monkey.

10. The soup is all gone, so there's no doubt it was delicious.

Focusing Talk:
Identifying What's Undoubtedly True... or Not

Read aloud "Me a Mess?" (see Resources, page 178). Reread the poem, substituting *not* for each *un-* prefix. Say, "*un-* is a prefix at the beginning of some words. It means *not.*" Then read aloud other poems, such as "My True Story" (page 179) or "P-E-A-C-E" (page 180) and invite children to respond "Undoubtedly it's true that…." if they think an idea could happen, or "It's undoubtedly false that…." if they think it could not be true.

Hands-On:
Playing Undoubtedly to Win

Help small groups play "Go Fish!" with two sets of letter or number cards. Dealer shuffles, deals seven cards to each, and lays remaining cards facedown. Players take turns asking for a card from the other. When asked, a player responds, "Undoubtedly, I (do/do not) have the (number or letter name)." Player asks again and gains a card or must "Go fish!", drawing from the stack. First empty-handed player undoubtedly wins.

WOW! Rhyme: **undoubtedly**

You are undoubtedly You.
And I am undoubtedly Me.
It's undoubtedly true:
I'm Me.
And you're You.
Could anyone doubt but agree?

Here's What It Means

noun: choices

Synonyms—*They have nearly the same meaning.*

all kinds	categories
all sorts	collection
all types	mixture
assortment	selection

Figuratively Speaking

the spice of life

Forms of *variety* to Share with 5s

variation (noun)
various (adjective)
vary (verb)

Talk & Share

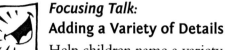

1. We have a variety of flowers in our garden.

2. The cafeteria offers a variety of desserts.

3. My box of crayons has a big variety of colors.

4. Though I've tried various flavors of ice cream, I still prefer vanilla.

5. The schedule for our music class may vary this week.

6. The color variations made the cloth look like a rainbow.

7. I tried on various shoes until I found the perfect pair.

8. Mom doesn't allow any variation in my bedtime.

9. The dog always chose the red ball from its variety of toys.

10. He likes to play various tricks on his sister.

Focusing Talk:
Adding a Variety of Details

Help children name a variety of details and characteristics, such as hair, eye color, dimples, or the shape of a nose, cheek, or chin, that make each person unlike any other. Provide blank pre-cut paper dolls. Ask children to tell why, other than that they're made of paper, the dolls do not look like the children. Help each child use crayons to give a doll a variety of details, features, and clothing to make it look like the real child.

Hands-On:
Tasting Apple Varieties

Provide three varieties of apples cut into small bites so that each child can taste each variety. Place a whole apple of each kind on its own paper plate. Have each child taste and then write "1" on the plate of his or her favorite variety, "3" on the least favorite, and "2" on the remaining plate. Have children mark a tally for each chosen apple, count the totals, and then place the apples in order to show children's tastes from most to least liked type of apple.

WOW! Rhyme: *variety*

I get a variety of choices.
I like it when I get to choose.
I like a variety
of foods
and of toys
and I *really* like choices of shoes!

AGE 6

- ☐ abundance
- ☐ accommodate
- ☐ acknowledge
- ☐ adapt
- ☐ advantage
- ☐ aggravate
- ☐ assertive
- ☐ assume
- ☐ authentic
- ☐ bewildered
- ☐ capacity
- ☐ clarify
- ☐ coincidence
- ☐ component
- ☐ confine
- ☐ conscious
- ☐ disastrous
- ☐ dominate

- ☐ elated
- ☐ hazardous
- ☐ intention
- ☐ legible
- ☐ leisure
- ☐ literally
- ☐ mutual
- ☐ obstacle
- ☐ perceive
- ☐ periodically
- ☐ perturbed
- ☐ ponder
- ☐ reluctant
- ☐ spontaneous
- ☐ summon
- ☐ thrifty
- ☐ vacant
- ☐ yield

Here's What It Means

noun: lots of

Synonyms—*They have nearly the same meaning.*

more than enough
plenty

Figuratively Speaking

bushels of; oodles and gobs;
more than one can handle

Forms of *abundance* to Share with 6s

abundant (adjective)
abundantly (adverb)

Talk & Share

1. Today I felt abundant joy.

2. I see an abundance of advertisements on TV.

3. This store has abundant choices of cereals.

4. I feel abundantly sorry for saying mean words.

5. I can read an abundant number of words now.

6. The water supply here is not abundant.

7. One week of abundant rain increased the lake's depth.

8. A coat can hide an abundance of things.

9. Our baby speaks an abundant number of sentences.

10. I felt abundant sadness when my grandpa passed away.

Focusing Talk: Noticing Abundances

Discuss how some things, such as blocks, sand grains, papers, beach pebbles, windows, and so on, can appear in abundance. Using a PMI (pluses, minuses, interesting) chart, help children list ideas as "Positive Abundance," "Negative Abundance," or "Interesting Abundance." Plus and Minus ideas may include toys, friends, freckles, happiness, sadness, or healthy foods. Snowflakes or paper clips might be listed as Interesting ideas.

Hands-On: Making an Abundance

Invite children to use scissors to change one sheet of scrap paper to an abundance of pieces of paper, or confetti. Encourage counting of the pieces as children cut. To repeat the activity, have children first plan how to cut through several thicknesses at a time for greater efficiency in making one piece of paper into a far greater number—an abundance. Children can give the confetti to owners of hamsters or other small animals.

WOW! Rhyme: **abundance**

We had an abundance of toys
till we shared with the girls and the boys.
We abundantly cared
and abundantly shared.
Now we all have an abundance of joys.

Here's What It Means

verb: to help make something fit

Synonyms—*They have nearly the same meaning.*

do a favor for	make space for
help out	offer service
help to fit in	provide for
make it easy for	supply

Figuratively Speaking

step up to the plate

Forms of *accommodate* to Share with 6s

accommodated (verb)

accommodates (verb)

accommodating (verb)

accommodations (noun)

Talk & Share

1. Our car accommodates four people.

2. We made time to accommodate our new classmate.

3. Our accommodations at the hotel were super.

4. My teacher accommodated me, because I was new.

5. My eyes had to accommodate the bright lights.

6. We are accommodating kids who want more lunch.

7. When Grandpa moves in, we will need to make some accommodations.

8. Dad rented a tent that will accommodate all of us.

9. I'll move over to accommodate one more person.

10. Stores accommodate customers by staying open at night.

Focusing Talk:
Accommodating Needs

Model a time when you were the "new kid on the block," how you felt, and specific needs you had. Help children follow your model to share experiences, such as needing a friend, feeling lonely or lost, not knowing what to expect, and so on. Help children list ways they might accommodate a new classmate. Ideas might include saying "hello" and "goodbye," inviting to play, sharing, or walking together in the hall.

Hands-On:
Noting Ways to Accommodate

Invite children to look for ways that the school and other places, such as stores, a playground, park, or library, accommodate persons who use walkers or who move about in specialized chairs. Invite partners to draw or cut out pictures of the accommodations and report their observations to the group. Ideas may include: ramp, lowered drinking fountain, wide halls and doors, lowered sink, hand rails, or an enlarged stall in the bathroom.

WOW! Rhyme: **accommodate**

Who will be accommodating?
Who'll be helping out?
Who'll be making extra space?
Who'll be singing out:
"Hey, hey, what do you say?"
"I'm hoping that you can come over
    to play!"

Here's What It Means

verb: to pay attention to

Synonyms—*They have nearly the same meaning.*

notice
recognize

Figuratively Speaking

sit up and take notice; give a high-five;
give a shout-out

Forms of *acknowledge* to Share with 6s

acknowledged (verb)
acknowledgement (noun)
acknowledges (verb)
acknowledging (verb)

Talk & Share

1. Let's acknowledge that it's okay to disagree about who should play.

2. My teacher calls each name to acknowledge who is here.

3. Mom's team lifted their coach in the air to acknowledge her super coaching.

4. I send a thank-you note to acknowledge every gift.

5. I like to be acknowledged.

6. Most people like it when others acknowledge them.

7. My aunt's acknowledgement is usually a big hug.

8. Grandma sometimes acknowledges extra helpers with money.

9. We acknowledged there were many toys to be put away.

10. Everyone is acknowledging my hard work.

Focusing Talk:
Being Acknowledged

Talk about times when you've been pleased or not pleased to gain acknowledgement. For example, share your feelings about acknowledgements for being on time versus being late or for having clean versus dirty hands. Help children complete a T-chart titled "Acknowledgements." Create two columns, one with a happy face heading and the other with a sad face. Help children list acknowledgements they've received or might receive.

Hands-On:
Preparing to Give Acknowledgements

Provide blue paper circles 3 inches in diameter; 2-inch-by-8½-inch blue paper strips; and gold stars or stickers and glitter, if desired. Invite each child to create a "blue ribbon" by gluing a circle atop the end of a paper strip. Children may want to decorate the strip and notch its bottom. Provide for children to make many "blue ribbons" and present them as acknowledgements when they notice positive behaviors of friends and family members.

WOW! Rhyme: **acknowledge**

They acknowledged it.
They did!
They did!
They acknowledged my work.
And I'm still a kid.

adapt (uh DAPT)

Here's What It Means
verb: to change to meet the need

Synonyms—*They have nearly the same meaning.*
alter
change
change up

Figuratively Speaking
shape up; get it together; make do

Forms of *adapt* to Share with 6s
adaptation (noun)
adapted (verb)
adapting (verb)
adaptive (adjective)
adapts (verb)

Talk & Share
1. It's hard to adapt to a time change.
2. I need to adapt to this cold weather.
3. My eyes adapted to the light.
4. Grandma says it took time to adapt to using a computer.
5. My great-grandpa is still adapting to our new baby.
6. I liked the movie adaptation of that book.
7. We are adapting dinner times around my game schedule.
8. It's hard to adapt to an earlier bedtime when school starts.
9. A chameleon is an adaptive creature because it adapts its color to new surroundings.
10. I had to adapt when we moved here.

Focusing Talk:
Noting Ways We Adapt
Help children name ways they have adapted or ways they may need to adapt to new situations. Examples may include a new sibling; a schedule change; a new chore; a time change in spring or fall; a move to a new home or city; a change in diet or medication; a loss of any kind; or learning a new skill. List children's ideas. Talk about the ease or difficulty involved in each adaptation. Post the list and add to it throughout the year.

Hands-On:
Picturing Animals' Adaptations
Invite children to work with family members, using magazines, newspapers, books, and the Internet, to draw or find pictures of animals that adapt to their surroundings. Examples might include whale's blubber or bear's fat as nourishment during winter; porcupine's quills for protection; and growth of hair by cats, dogs, and horses for winter warmth. Help children glean and collate pictures to illustrate a book titled "Some Ways Animals Adapt."

WOW! Rhyme: ***adapt***

I adapt.
I change
like all people do.
But sometimes it's *hard* to adapt—
It's true!

Here's What It Means

noun: something that's very helpful

Another Meaning

noun: a point scored in tennis after a tie

Synonyms—*They have nearly the same meaning.*

benefit
big help
profit

Figuratively Speaking

one up on; an edge up

Forms of *advantage* to Share with 6s

advantageous (adjective)
disadvantage (noun)

Talk & Share

1. My cousin's advantage is that she's older than the rest of us.

2. I'll have an advantage in getting home earlier than usual.

3. There are advantages in being able to run fast and jump high.

4. No one took advantage of my being a new student.

5. She knows the rules, and that's definitely an advantage.

6. Mem had the disadvantage of having no boots or umbrella.

7. My good eyesight is an advantage in the woods.

8. We found an advantageous place to get a super view.

9. I was listening, so I had an advantage when the timer rang.

10. Boots and mittens are advantages when playing in the snow.

Focusing Talk:
Considering Advantages

Draw a T-chart to note advantages that are factual versus opinions. For example, using "Fact" and "Opinion" as headings, consider carrying an umbrella. Help children list a fact, such as "keeps you dry," compared to an opinion, such as "it might rain." List additional facts and opinions for ideas, such as actual and suggested advantages of bringing lunch to school, walking to school, or usir an alarm clock.

Hands-On:
Picturing Safety Advantages for Travel

Share "Alas!" (see Resources, page 175). Discuss why a seat belt is an advantage to Jill and how she and Jack might have traveled in this poem. Invite children to consider how else Jack and Jill might travel and which safety advantages they might want (boat—life jacket; motorcycle—helmet; etc.). Help children cut and glue pictures to depict safety advantages for various ways of traveling. Compile pages to create a book titled "Safe Travels."

WOW! Rhyme: **advantage**

A clock is an advantage
when I want to know the time.
But Grandpa's clock
is a disadvantage—
It jolts me with its chime.

Here's What It Means

verb: to make worse

Synonyms—*They have nearly the same meaning.*

annoy
burden down with
make more difficult
upset

Forms of *aggravate* to Share with 6s

aggravated (adjective, verb)
aggravates (verb)
aggravating (adjective, verb)
aggravation (noun)

Talk & Share

1. Wind can aggravate allergies.

2. A shoe is a real aggravation for a sore toe.

3. Mom thinks my brother and I aggravate each other.

4. It's aggravating when someone interrupts me.

5. Scientists now know that global warming is aggravated by smog.

6. Any noise aggravates my grandpa when he's sleeping.

7. Those TV ads aggravated my aunt.

8. My dad thinks rainy days aggravate the pain in his shoulder.

9. It aggravates me when people make noise chewing gum.

10. Maybe we should ask if something is aggravating Mia.

Focusing Talk:
Discussing Aggravating Behaviors

Talk about behaviors that may aggravate others. Help children make a T-chart titled "Aggravating Behaviors" for listing such behaviors in the left-hand column. Talk about ways to speak or act assertively, without being rude, to avoid becoming aggravated by another's behavior. List in the right-hand column one or more helpful ideas, such as: walk away from annoying noise, cover ears, count silently, or ask someone to please stop.

Hands-On:
Surveying Aggravations to Senses

Have each child choose one of the five senses and draw its feature, such as eyes for seeing, nose for smelling, and so on. Invite children to survey ten people to tally aggravations. For example, children might ask, "What, if anything, aggravates your eyes?" Children make a tally mark for each named item, such as car headlights or chemicals in the air in a carpet store. Have children report their survey results to the whole group.

WOW! Rhyme: *aggravate*

I felt so aggravated—
all upset and so annoyed.
'Twas such an aggravation
when my bedroom got destroyed.
But my puppy didn't mean to cause me
aggravating stress.
So bye-bye aggravation!
We are cleaning up this mess.

Here's What It Means

adjective: able to say how you feel about something

Synonyms—*They have nearly the same meaning.*

able to express oneself   speaking boldly
acting confident   speaking out
declaring one's ideas

Figuratively Speaking

stick up for yourself; stand up and be counted; stand your ground; not get pushed around

Forms of *assertive* to Share with 6s

assert (verb)
asserted (verb)
asserting (verb)
assertiveness (noun)
asserts (verb)

Talk & Share

1. I try to be assertive without being rude.

2. Our coach was assertive about the rules.

3. Mom says I need to show more assertiveness.

4. He asserted his innocence.

5. My dog is too assertive to get bullied.

6. Our cat asserts herself when the dog comes near.

7. Our baby is walking now and asserting her independence.

8. I can't assert an idea if I don't believe in it.

9. Aunt Cecelia asserted her need for privacy.

10. I must be assertive so that my friend will know how I feel.

Focusing Talk:
Being Assertive to Get Needs Met

Help children list some basic needs all people share. Examples might include: shelter, water, safety, love, friendship, air, comfort, food, rest or sleep, hope, freedom, space, cooperation, joy, trust, affection. Invite discussion about ways to be assertive to get a basic need met. For example, one might say "No!" to assert a need for safety or freedom, or ask for a pillow or blanket to meet a need for comfort, rest, or sleep.

Hands-On:
Dramatizing Assertiveness

Ask family members to help children practice assertiveness as appropriate at home. Then have children bring in pictures that show a living being who has a basic need that's not being met. Examples might include persons or animals who look tired, cold, or hungry. Have partners take turns dramatizing the needy character or the needy helper being assertive in asking for something to meet a need. Talk about whether each situation might actually happen.

WOW! Rhyme: **assertive**

Sometimes I act assertive
and assertively sing a song.
It helps me feel assertive
if a bully should come along.

assume (uh SUUM)

Here's What It Means

verb: to think you know something

Synonyms—*They have nearly the same meaning.*

believe   suppose
guess   understand

Figuratively Speaking

take for granted

Forms of *assume* to Share with 6s

assumed (verb)
assumes (verb)
assuming (verb)
assumption (noun)
assumptions (noun)

Talk & Share

1. Grandpa was right to assume we'd want pizza.

2. I assumed you didn't invite me, but I was wrong.

3. It's my assumption that I won't like what's in this box.

4. My assumptions are sometimes right!

5. Aunt Tara assumes we can spend the night.

6. I am assuming you want to switch channels.

7. Dad said he didn't want to assume which color I'd like.

8. When I graduate from high school, it is assumed I'll go to college.

9. I learned that making assumptions can lead to trouble!

10. Let's ask before we make any assumptions.

Focusing Talk: Making Assumptions... or Not

Tell about making an assumption without fact-checking. For example, you may have assumed a friend was angry but learned later that he hadn't known you were nearby, or a time you assumed that a bulb had burned out but found that the lamp's cord wasn't plugged into the outlet. Help children tell of times they or family members have made assumptions but later learned details that could have helped them avoid extra work or hurt feelings.

Hands-On: Making Assumptions and Checking Them Out

Provide writing paper. List possible model words and read the words until children can recognize each. Have groups of three take turns so that one child is the writer, one hears the writer's whispered secret, and one reads what is written and makes an assumption to predict a word the writer will write in the blank. Help the writer to write, "(writer's first name) wants to _____." and then whisper one word, such as *sleep* or *eat*. The third child then makes an assumption before the writer writes the word.

WOW! Rhyme: *assume*

I'm assuming you'll be helpful.
I'm assuming you'll be kind.
I'm assuming my assumptions
match the things you had in mind.

Here's What It Means

adjective: the real thing

Synonyms—*They have nearly the same meaning.*

accurate   reliable
actual   true to form
genuine   valid
not a fake

Figuratively Speaking

the real McCoy

Forms of *authentic* to Share with 6s

authenticate (verb)
authentically (adverb)
authenticity (noun)

Talk & Share

1. My grandma has an authentic arrowhead.
2. My baseball hat is an authentic team hat.
3. If it cuts glass, it is an authentic diamond.
4. Maybe someone will authenticate my story.
5. I have an authentic excuse for being tardy.
6. Your look of surprise was truly authentic!
7. Is your stamp collection authentic?
8. How can we check the authenticity of this souvenir?
9. Dad has an authentic antique car.
10. Some seemed authentically sad to leave.

Focusing Talk:
Exploring an Authentic Friendship

Talk about how you and a close or authentic friend are always ready to help one another. Tell about things you like to do together and ways you help each other. Invite children to follow your model to talk about the qualities of an authentic friendship of theirs, without telling the person's name. List children's ideas. Discuss behaviors, such as gossiping, calling names, or saying unkind words, that describe an other than authentic friendship.

Hands-On:
Sorting for Authentic Treasures

Collect trinkets and such items as an interesting pencil, sticker, marble, keychain, or notepad. Then help children draw or cut out pictures of those real items. Stage a hunt for "Authentic Treasures" by hiding the pictures and real objects. Invite children to search for authentic items. Announce each "find" in sentences, such as "I found an authentic (item name)," or "My treasure is not an authentic (item name). It's a picture."

WOW! Rhyme: **authentic**

My pet is authentic.
Not plastic.
Not fake.
It's real!
Its authentic!
My pet is a snake!

Here's What It Means

adjective: totally surprised and confused
verb: to be surprised or confused

Synonyms—*They have nearly the same meaning.*

all mixed up   dumbfounded
baffled   puzzled
dazed

Figuratively Speaking

at a loss; befuddled; discombobulated; in the dark; in a fog; flummoxed; mind-boggling

Forms of *bewildered* to Share with 6s

bewilder (verb)
bewildering (adjective, verb)
bewilderment (noun)
bewilders (verb)

Talk & Share

1. I felt bewildered when you didn't say hello to me.

2. It bewilders me when people choose to fight.

3. He looked bewildered until we asked him to play with us.

4. Our dog looks at us with bewilderment when we get out our suitcases.

5. We felt bewildered when our key didn't work in the lock.

6. My big sister's homework bewildered me.

7. No computer seems to bewilder my grandpa.

8. His cell phone sometimes bewilders my dad.

9. A book can look bewildering until I open it.

10. Grandma says this huge store is bewildering her.

Focusing Talk: Discussing Bewilderment

Tell children about something that bewilders you. For example, you might tell how you find it bewildering that people can forget to turn off a light or TV when leaving a room. Help children discuss things that bewilder them. Then focus on other people's feelings by sharing a behavior you did that bewildered someone in your life. Help children follow your model to name times when their own behaviors were bewildering to others.

Hands-On: Making Cards about Bewilderments

Have children make greeting cards by folding half-sheets of paper. Help children draw a bewildered-looking face on the card's cover. Provide old magazines and newspapers for children to cut out and glue, inside their cards, a picture of a person's or animal's action that could cause another to feel bewildered. Examples might be a dog digging a hole, a baby spilling a drink, or a dark computer screen. Have children share cards at home.

WOW! Rhyme: **bewildered**

It bewilders me
how owies
and these boo-boos came my way.
I'm bewildered
and I'm puzzled.
Might it be how rough I play?

(*Note:* You may want to share similar language in the poem "Skerbonker Doodles!" See Resources, page 180.)

capacity (kuh PAS i tee)

Here's What It Means

noun: ability to hold or to do something

Synonyms—*They have nearly the same meaning.*

size
how much

Talk & Share

1. This swing's capacity is one person.

2. Our car's capacity is four people in seat belts.

3. The sign says this room has a capacity to hold 100.

4. The baby's cup has a capacity of just four ounces.

5. I wonder if that tiny car has a capacity of one or two passengers.

6. My water jug has a 10-ounce capacity.

7. The sign says the parking garage is full to capacity.

8. My friend and I have the capacity to help you do that job.

9. I've filled this bucket to its capacity.

10. What is this stadium's capacity?

Focusing Talk: Exploring Capacities

Tell children that the word *capacity* is used to refer to a person's ability to do something and also to tell how much a container holds. Help children name abilities they own—such as making a bed, tying shoes, riding a bike, or making a sandwich—as you list their ideas. At another time, invite children to spend a full week studying capacity labels on containers and products at home and in stores. Help children report their findings.

Hands-On: Experimenting to Find Capacity

Provide partners a paper towel, a small container of water, spoon, and pencil and paper. Tell children they are to find the paper towel's capacity to absorb or hold water. Ask partners to lay the towel on a protected surface and take turns spooning water onto the paper. The other person tallies the number of spoonfuls the paper can absorb before it is soaked to capacity. Children will find that puddles will form once the towel has reached its capacity.

WOW! Rhyme: **capacity**

His capacity for yelling
and screaming is small.
But Grandpa's capacity
for hugging
is "tall"!

Here's What It Means

verb: to make clear

Synonyms—*They have nearly the same meaning.*

clear up   point out
demonstrate   show
make simple

Forms of *clarify* to Share with 6s

clarification (noun)
clarified (verb)
clarifies (verb)
clarifying (verb)

Talk & Share

1. I want to clarify what I meant.

2. Let's wait till we get some clarification.

3. Dad clarified that he wanted my room cleaned now.

4. I like it when Mom clarifies what she means before I begin a job.

5. Nobody clarified how we were to get to the park.

6. I will be clarifying what I mean if you can wait a second.

7. Sometimes a task needs lots of clarification.

8. Could you please clarify how long I should practice?

9. I understand, now that you have clarified the directions.

10. I asked her to clarify this problem for me.

Focusing Talk:
Clarifying a Request

Without pointing, ask children to go sit *there*. Children should note how the word *there* needs clarification. Invite ways to clarify the request, such as you could point, or you could say words that specify a location. Children might also ask questions to rule in or rule out ideas about the meaning of *there*. Help children identify times when clarification is useful and helpful. This is a good time to introduce the word *vague* to mean unclear.

Hands-On:
Giving Clarification

Ask children's family members to draw a simple map of the interior layout of their homes. Show a similar map of your home and, without pointing, tell about where in your home you generally eat, sleep, read, or do other activities. Help children note the need for you to clarify exactly *where* you mean. Then invite partners to similarly share their home maps with vague versus clarified information about their activities in their homes.

WOW! Rhyme: **clarify**

What's that?
What's that you say?
Please clarify
what you would like—
then we can go and play.

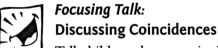
Here's What It Means

noun: things that surprise us when they happen in the same time or space

Synonyms—*They have nearly the same meaning.*

chance happenings
unexpected happenings at the same time
unplanned happenings at the same time

Figuratively Speaking

lucky break; stroke of luck; fluke

Forms of *coincidence* to Share with 6s

coincide (verb)
coincidental (adjective)
coincidentally (adverb)

Talk & Share

1. It's a coincidence that you and I have the same birthday.

2. We are coincidentally reading the same book.

3. Coincidentally, we both have rescued kittens.

4. It's no coincidence when twins have the same birthday!

5. It was coincidental that we had the same foods in our lunches.

6. Our costumes were coincidentally from the same store.

7. It was coincidental that we arrived at the same time.

8. It's a coincidence because we didn't plan for this to happen.

9. What a coincidence! The two of them had studied at the same college.

10. We coincidentally ordered the same dessert.

Focusing Talk: Discussing Coincidences

Tell children about a coincidental experience, such as a time when you called or e-mailed someone who was about to contact you or when you and a friend had the same idea to do something. Help children discern between a real coincidence and a fantasy or a construed situation. Then invite children to be on the lookout for coincidences they or family members experience. Ask children to use *coincidence* or its forms in sentences to share.

Hands-On: Testing for Coincidental Choices

Help partners lay out twenty counters beside an empty container. Tell partners they have twenty tries to make the same choice. Have each partner secretly write an alphabet letter on a scrap of paper. As one child reveals a secret letter, the partner places one counter in the container to show one try. If partners coincidentally write the same letter, have them record a tally mark. Have partners tell if, in twenty tries, they coincidentally wrote the same letter.

WOW! Rhyme: *coincidence*

It's such a coincidence—
it happened today.
I wanted a friend.
And *you* came to play!

Here's What It Means

noun: one part of a whole

Synonyms—*They have nearly the same meaning.*

detail   portion
fraction of   section
parcel   unit
piece

Talk & Share

1. Some of the components are missing from this kit.

2. Let's build it one component at a time.

3. We need to look at all the components in this situation.

4. The back pocket is one component of these pants that I dislike.

5. One component of a book is its cover.

6. The universe is made up of many components.

7. Safety is just one component of the trip that concerns me.

8. Surely there are more components still in the box.

9. This adds another component to our morning routine.

10. Rest is one component of good health.

Focusing Talk:
Discussing Components of Peaceful Behavior

Read and sing "P-E-A-C-E" (see Resources, page 180). Help children talk about times when they have noticed their own or another person's peaceful behavior that used one or more components mentioned in the poem (mouth, hands, feet). Invite children to use words, drawings, and pictures to create an ongoing bulletin board display that captures ways people can and do use each of the three body components to make peace.

Hands-On:
Exploring Components of Good Health

Talk about components of good overall health. Examples may include exercise, healthy eating, sleep, medical checkups, daily tooth care, or making friendships. Help a group focus on each component and report back to the whole group. Groups might compile a book, demonstrate dental hygiene or exercise, explain the food triangle, talk about doctor visits, share ways to make and keep friends, or use clocks to show healthy sleep habits.

WOW! Rhyme: *component*

Too many components!
And too many charts!
Instructions!
Components!
There are too many parts!

Here's What It Means

verb: to keep to one space or idea

Synonyms—*They have nearly the same meaning.*

border

keep within a boundary

limit in some way

shut up in a space

Forms of *confine* to Share with 6s

confined (adjective)

confines (verb)

confining (adjective)

Talk & Share

1. We confine food to the kitchen at my house.

2. I tried to color within the confined spaces.

3. Dad confined us to our rooms.

4. I feel confined because I've grown too big for this jacket.

5. We can mark lines to confine the relay racers.

6. Police put up cones as barriers to confine the traffic.

7. Do our rules seem too confining?

8. We put up a fence to confine our dog.

9. The bulletin board confines our display.

10. Our activities may be confined by the weather.

Focusing Talk: Discussing Confining Rules

Help children name rules and expectations they experience at home or in school and possible reasons for each. Talk about how some rules may seem confining, while others may not. Encourage children to use sentences to tell which rules they think are confining and why. Then invite discussion about rules and expectations that confine adults, such as rules for driving, getting senior discounts, voting, getting jobs, or rules in the workplace.

Hands-On: Choosing Borders to Confine

Provide half sheets of manila paper for children to draw self-portraits. Invite children to think about alphabet letters, numbers, and geometric shapes they know how to write or draw. Model using one or a combination of such characters to create a framing border. Talk about how a border frames and confines a picture as it adds to the picture's visual appeal. Invite children to create borders that confine and frame their self-portraits.

WOW! Rhyme: **confine**

If dogs could talk,

then a dog might say:

"That's way too confining!

This dog wants to play.

A crate is confining;

a fence is no fun.

Confine me?

Please don't!

This dog wants to run!"

Here's What It Means

adjective: being aware

Synonyms—*They have nearly the same meaning.*

alert to	intended to
awake	knowing about
having noticed	meaning to

Figuratively Speaking

clued in; tuned in

Forms of *conscious* to Share with 6s

consciously (adverb)

consciousness (noun)

unconsciously (adverb)

Talk & Share

1. I am conscious of needing more time to do my chores.

2. I said that unconsciously, so I hope you'll forgive me.

3. I trust you are consciously doing your best.

4. We need to be conscious of the time.

5. Mom says we need more consciousness of rules.

6. Grandpa asked us to be conscious about the need to be kind.

7. Libraries expect readers to be conscious of deadlines.

8. It's hard to act consciously when I'm tired.

9. He is conscious of his mistake.

10. I wasn't conscious of any pain.

Focusing Talk:
Sorting Out Consciousness

Create a T-chart titled "Behaviors" with headings "Conscious" and "Unconscious." Help children discuss and list behaviors they and others do. Talk about how many behaviors, such as following rules or even making rules, may fit in both columns. Encourage healthy debate and acceptance of differences if disagreements occur around whether a behavior, such as foot tapping, is conscious or unconscious.

Hands-On:
Dramatizing Consciousness

Invite partners to mime short skits in which one child is consciously trying to do something well while the other child seems to be doing the wrong thing, but unconsciously. For example, one child might be trying to sit up straight while another slouches without care, or one might consciously work to walk a balance beam while the other jumps on and off the beam. Ask others to use *conscious* and its forms to name and discuss the activity.

WOW! Rhyme: ***conscious***

I'm conscious of chores

and conscious of time

but, also,

I'm conscious

that I'd rather climb!

Here's What It Means

adjective: awful loss

Synonyms—*They have nearly the same meaning.*

destructive	terrible
loss with great suffering	total failure
shocking	total loss

Forms of *disastrous* to Share with 6s

disaster (noun, adjective)
disastrously (adverb)

Talk & Share

1. There was a disastrous mess in the kitchen.

2. I hope this game will not end disastrously.

3. Fighting was a disastrous way to handle the problem.

4. Someone did a disastrous job of painting the fence.

5. My little brother made my room a disaster zone.

6. We tried but failed disastrously.

7. The whole neighborhood looked disastrous after the storm.

8. The dog left disastrous surprises throughout the house.

9. By the time we got home, our paper maps looked like a disaster had hit them.

10. Our baby's high chair was a disaster after dinner.

Focusing Talk:
Identifying Disastrous Situations

Talk about how people tend to use the word *disastrous* to mean really messed up, like a bedroom or a friendship that gets messed up, but the word is also used to mean totally destroyed, such as when homes and businesses are destroyed. List children's ideas around natural versus human-made disastrous situations and some causes. For example, natural causes include hurricanes, tornadoes, fire from lightning strikes, and earthquakes.

Hands-On:
Sorting for Two Types of Disasters

Provide magazines and newspapers for children to clip pictures of natural disasters and pictures of human-made disastrous situations, such as a messy bedroom or bathroom, a yard filled with trash, a totally messy desk, a baby's dinner mess, or people having a heated argument. Have children dictate captions for each picture to create two books titled "Natural Disastrous Situations" and "Human-made Disastrous Situations."

WOW! Rhyme: *disastrous*

Last night was disastrous.

I fell out of bed.

I fell out of bed and bumped my head.

A bump on my head turned purple
   and red.

Dad called up the doctor.

The doctor said,

"It's only a bump. Go climb into bed."

Last night was disastrous...

and thankfully, a dream.

Here's What It Means

verb: to take charge

Synonyms—*They have nearly the same meaning.*

control   stand out from the rest
lead   take over
rule

Figuratively Speaking

call the shots; be in the driver's seat;
lay down the law; rule the roost

Forms of *dominate* to Share with 6s

dominant (adjective)
dominated (adjective, verb)
dominates (verb)
dominating (adjective, verb)

Talk & Share

1. I like it when no one dominates a meeting so that everyone gets to talk.

2. My dog dominates our cat.

3. Let's see if anyone tries to dominate the meeting.

4. I like to dominate my family when it comes to picking TV shows.

5. There are more brown-eyed people in the world, so brown eyes are dominant.

6. Was anyone acting too dominant during recess?

7. My friend dominated our discussion.

8. Somebody keeps dominating the conversation.

9. Our survey found that macaroni and cheese is the dominant food choice.

10. Chocolate chip cookies dominated when folks were asked their favorite dessert.

Focusing Talk:
Considering Domination

Read "Who's the Boss?" (see Resources, page 182) before discussing how it feels to be in charge of oneself. Ask children to tell about times they have had to "boss" or dominate their tongues, hands, or feet to prevent getting into trouble. Talk about times when it is a strength to be dominating or to be the leader versus times when someone acts dominating over others and it feels like the person is being bossy.

Hands-On:
Surveying Eye-color Dominance

Tell children the scientific fact that more people have brown eyes than blue eyes. Help each child make a T-chart to record their own survey. Have children fold a 4-inch-by-6-inch index card such that each half is 3 inches, open the card, and color a brown strip across top left and a blue strip at top right. Ask children to survey folks for one week and mark a tally for each blue-eyed or brown-eyed person. Help children total and compare tallies.

> *WOW!* Rhyme: **dominate**
>
> You are in charge of you.
> And I am in charge of me.
> So no one dominates us both—
> You will, of course, agree.

Here's What It Means

adjective: full of joy

Synonyms—*They have nearly the same meaning.*

excited   uplifted

lively   very happy

overjoyed

Figuratively Speaking

jumping for joy; pumped; tickled pink; sitting on top of the world; on cloud nine; happy as a clam at high tide

Forms of *elated* to Share with 6s

elating (verb)

elation (noun)

Talk & Share

1. I'm elated that you came to visit.
2. People often feel and act elated at birthday parties.
3. Mom finds it elating when we do chores done any reminders.
4. Can you remember the last time you felt elated?
5. Aunt Zoe said she was elated to see me.
6. Our dog is elated when we come home.
7. Our dog is not elated when she sees us pack for a trip.
8. I was elated to hear the sound of music.
9. Our elation ended when all the balloons popped.
10. This should elate you and lift your spirits a bit.

Focusing Talk: Feeling Elated

Talk about times you have felt elated and why. Examples might include a time when you found something you had lost or a time when you won a prize. Encourage children to identify, list, and talk about times when they have felt elation. Help children recognize, compare, and discuss how differently two people can feel about the same idea, such as a birthday, holiday, or giving or receiving a gift. Talk about elation versus feeling pleased.

Hands-On: Capturing Times of Elation

Take photos of children or invite them to bring from home a photo that shows their being elated. Photos may include family members or friends. For preservation, have children use a drop of glue to attach photos to drawing paper. Have children use pen or black marker to personalize their pages with their names and, perhaps, a border to frame each photo. Photocopy pages and compile for a book. Make copies for each classmate to take home.

WOW! Rhyme: **elated**

I'm elated!

It's inflated.

It's as full as it can be!

I'm elated

It's inflated…

Now it's gonna cushion me!

Here's What It Means

adjective: extremely dangerous

Synonyms—*They have nearly the same meaning.*

damaging   risky
daring   unhealthy
harmful

Figuratively Speaking

chancy; dicey; slippery; thorny; out on a limb; skating on thin ice

Form of *hazardous* to Share with 6s

hazard (noun)

Talk & Share

1. Chemicals can be hazardous.

2. Smoking is known to be hazardous to one's health.

3. That road is hazardous to drive on because of its many holes.

4. There don't seem to be any hazards ahead.

5. Mom seems to think it's hazardous to let me stay up late.

6. Riding without a seat belt is hazardous and illegal.

7. Police often put orange cones around a hazardous area.

8. Lack of sleep can be hazardous to good health.

9. Driving too fast is hazardous to the driver and others.

10. I stand back if I see that there are hazards ahead.

Focusing Talk:
Discussing Possible Hazards

Read "Alas!" (see Resources, page 175). Talk about how seat belts help prevent hazards when traveling. Reread the poem to substitute protective gear, such as a helmet, shin pads, or a life vest. Help children name other physical activities and times when each may present a hazard. Examples can include swimming alone or when tired, walking at night without reflective clothing, lifting heavy objects, or sweating without drinking water.

Hands-On:
Creating Signs to Warn of Hazards

Share Internet sites, such as http://www.compliancesigns.com/DOT_Placards.shtml or http://www.usa-traffic-signs.com. Note shapes (usually triangle or rectangle) and purposes of signs to signal caution or note a hazard. You may want to learn more about safety signage at http://www.osha.gov/SLTC/hazardcommunications. Provide paper and markers for children to create signs to warn of a hazardous situation at school or at home.

WOW! Rhyme: **hazardous**

What a bad choice.
'Twas a hazardous trick—
for Jack to jump over
a candlestick.
'Twas a hazardous thing for Jack to do.
I'd never do that.
Would you?
Would you?

Here's What It Means

noun: plan

Synonyms—*They have nearly the same meaning.*

aim   meaning
goal   purpose

Forms of *intention* to Share with 6s

intend (verb)
intended (verb)
intending (verb)
intends (verb)
intentional (adjective)
intentionally (adverb)

Talk & Share

1. It's my intention to do the right thing.

2. I didn't intend to hit anything with the rock.

3. Moira intends to finish high school and then go to college.

4. It seemed like her hurtful words were intentional.

5. We intended to take foods Grammie would like.

6. Some thought she'd broken the pencil intentionally.

7. We're intending to decorate tonight.

8. My intention is to drink more water each day.

9. Did both of you intend to wear red today?

10. Dad says his intention is to arrive a bit early.

Focusing Talk: Talking about Intentions

Read "A Mighty Knight" (see Resources, page 178). Tell children you had two intentions in mind as you read aloud this poem, and that one intention was to enjoy a funny poem. Ask if this poem worked for that intention.

Tell how you also intended for children to hear words that rhyme with *knight*, and ask whether this poem worked for that intention. Help children use *intention* or a form of the word to restate your two intentions in sharing this poem (enjoy a funny poem; hear rhyming words).

Hands-On: Remembering Intentions

Provide three short string strips for each child. Ask children to think of three things they intend to do after school or at home tonight and stroke one string as a reminder. Invite children to take strings home to share with family members how a string helps them remember an intention. Have children return the strings the next day and talk about their three intentions from the night before. Repeat for three new intentions each day of the week.

WOW! Rhyme: **intention**

He says he intends to be polite.
He says he doesn't intend to fight.
He says he intends to take a light.
He says his intention is to win tonight.
We hear his intention; we think he's right.
We think he'll dress as a mighty knight.

Here's What It Means

adjective: easy to read

Synonyms—*They have nearly the same meaning.*

carefully printed
clearly written
written neatly

Figuratively Speaking

not like chicken scratch

Forms of *legible* to Share with 6s

illegible (adjective)
legibility (noun)
legibly (adjective)

Talk & Share

1. It's important to write your name legibly.

2. The sign on the door was illegible.

3. My brother writes legibly in manuscript and in cursive.

4. The dollar amount on the check was illegible.

5. We couldn't make out the illegible writing on the treasure chest.

6. The label is quite legible, actually.

7. Grandpa says a tiny font on the computer screen is illegible to his aging eyes.

8. He likes the legibility of very large print.

9. Do you think you can print so it's legible?

10. I think my printing is totally legible.

Focusing Talk: Discussing Legibility

Print several children's names across the chalkboard such that every name is totally illegible. Ask children to stand by the chalkboard beneath their names. Help children use forms of *legible* to tell how they're feeling about your request. Repeat the activity to write some names legibly and some illegibly. Discuss times, such as when filling out checks or passport applications, when writing legibly is extremely important.

Hands-On: Writing Legible Notes

Pair children such that *both* can successfully read and write a list of words you present them. Help partners use the word list to write one-sentence notes to each other and sign their names. Have each pair swap notes with another pair of children, read aloud to each other, and then talk about each note's legibility or illegibility. Repeat to increase legibility, if needed. Re-partner children with new word lists.

> WOW! Rhyme: **legible**
>
> It's legible.
> It is.
> I printed my best.
> I printed it legibly—
> but then it got messed.

Here's What It Means

noun: free time
adjective: free or unscheduled

Synonyms—*They have nearly the same meaning.*

ease   spare time
recess   time off
restful time   unscheduled time

Figuratively Speaking

R&R; time to chill out; down time

Form of *leisure* to Share with 6s

leisurely (adverb)

Talk & Share

1. Dad and I had some leisure time together.
2. Aunt Paula asked what I'd like to do in my leisure time today.
3. We can leave at your leisure.
4. Our Sunday afternoons are spent leisurely at my house.
5. Grandpa was wearing a leisure suit in that old picture.
6. Mom's idea of leisure is to curl up and read.
7. There's no leisure time in our schedule tomorrow.
8. Let's do that tomorrow for leisure.
9. I like leisurely activities on the weekend.
10. Aunt Clara came over to join us for leisure time.

Focusing Talk:
Choosing Leisurely Activities

Invite children to name their favorite leisure activities. List each idea, and introduce or review the expression "Different strokes for different folks" where children's ideas about leisure differ. Have children use tally marks to show each activity's popularity. Help children use their totals to make a bar graph on chart paper. List activities up the left side (Y axis) and color a space across the graph (X axis) for each child favoring that activity.

Hands-On:
Erasing Boredom During Leisure Time

Provide each child four 3-inch-by-5-inch index cards, a hole punch, and string. Have children draw or cut and glue pictures or use words to depict on each a leisure activity they would enjoy doing alone. You may want to invite exclusion of the use of TV and electronics. Help children punch one corner of each activity card and join them with string. Invite children to hang their "Leisure Time Suggestions" in their room or another area at home.

WOW! Rhyme: *leisure*

You use leisure time for walking.
I use leisure time for chalking.
You find sidewalks good for walking.
I find sidewalks great for chalking!

Here's What It Means

adverb: actually; exactly as said

Synonyms—*They have nearly the same meaning.*

actual words   factual

exactly as said   really what the words mean

Figuratively Speaking

strictly speaking; really now

Form of *literally* to Share with 6s

literal (adjective)

Talk & Share

1. We are literally out of gas.

2. It's literally not my fault.

3. Amelia Bedelia is funny when she thinks of a literal meaning.

4. Nothing I said should be taken literally.

5. Mom said my room was literally a pigpen.

6. Literally speaking, you are all wet.

7. My dad was literally too tired to stand.

8. At first, I took it literally when Grannie said she's pinching pennies.

9. My friend is literally out in left field.

10. The nurse was literally as gentle as a lamb.

Focusing Talk:
Speaking Literally... or Figuratively?

Share a book about Amelia Bedelia (see Resources, page 173). Discuss Amelia's literal understandings of words and phrases, which are meant to be understood for their figurative meanings. Invite children to tell the literal and figurative meanings of other expressions, such as "time flies," "on pins and needles," or "saved by the bell." Note that a figurative expression may be referred to as figurative language, a cliché, or an idiom.

Hands-On:
Dramatizing Language Literally and Figuratively

Invite children to dramatize the literal and figurative meanings for "keep it under your hat," "toe the line," "keep an eye out for it," "all thumbs," "a meeting of minds," "pulling my leg," and other expressions (see the Figurative Language index, page 188). Encourage children to listen for such language uses by family members. At another time, invite children to use drawings to show the literal and figurative meanings of clichés.

WOW! Rhyme: *literally*

I took things literally.
Back then, I did.
I believed whatever—
when I was a kid.

Here's What It Means

adjective: similar

Synonyms—*They have nearly the same meaning.*

agreement
connected
in common
joint

related
same relationship
shared

Figuratively Speaking

give and take; one for all and all for one

Form of *mutual* to Share with 6s

mutually (adverb)

Talk & Share

1. Bo and I learned that we have a mutual friend.

2. Humans have mutual needs for love and security.

3. Uncle Fred wants to meet people with hobbies mutual to his own.

4. We are mutually concerned about being safe.

5. My family members share a mutual bathroom.

6. Most kids in my class have mutual interests in sports.

7. I'd say the feeling of wanting to be right is mutual.

8. My friends and I have mutual interests in books.

9. Everyone in my family uses a mutual cell phone account.

10. What mutual interests do you two have?

Focusing Talk:
Listing Ideas that are Mutually Exclusive

Tell children that mutually exclusive actions are things, such as eating and sleeping, standing still and walking, giggling and swallowing, behaving and misbehaving, that can't happen at the same time. Invite children to dictate complete sentences, such as "Standing and sitting are mutually exclusive actions," as you write the list. At another time, you may want to have children illustrate the front and back of paper to show more mutually exclusive actions.

Hands-On:
Finding Mutual Interests

Have children draw three circles on a sheet of paper. Ask children to draw one picture (or glue photos) inside each circle to illustrate three different activities they enjoy. Invite children to take their paper and walk around the room until a leader says, "Stop to find a friend with whom you have a mutual interest." Then ask partners, "What mutual interest do you have?" Repeat for children to find other friends with mutual interests.

WOW! Rhyme: **mutual**

I love Dad
and Dad loves me.
We love each other
mutually.

Here's What It Means

noun: something that blocks the way

Synonyms—*They have nearly the same meaning.*

ban   obstruction
curb   roadblock

Figuratively Speaking

a hitch; stumbling block; brick wall

Talk & Share

1. Those trees present an obstacle to seeing the lake.

2. I need to study now to prevent obstacles when I'm in high school.

3. It's a fire hazard to have obstacles in front of doorways.

4. My door's deadbolt is an obstacle to folks who don't live here.

5. There's an obstacle in the sink drain.

6. That building is an obstacle that prevents my view of the playground.

7. Let's move these obstacles so we can get through the room.

8. Rain can present all sorts of obstacles for drivers.

9. Potholes in the street are obstacles for all vehicles.

10. Cones in the street present obstacles when I'm riding my bike.

Focusing Talk:
Pantomiming Obstacles

Invite partners to pantomime skits for classmates to name a task that one partner attempts to do and the obstacle the other child puts in the way. For example, a child might try to pass a yard where a barking dog is the obstacle, reach for a book on a shelf where a table is an obstacle, or try to go outside on a snowy day but a frozen-shut door is an obstacle. Help children use *obstacle* to ask and answer questions to identify each skit.

Hands-On:
Considering Obstacles

Provide trays with some packing popcorn or confetti. Ask partners to move the popcorn from the tray to a paper bag. Help children create a T-chart with columns titled "Obstacle" and "Solution" to list each obstacle they meet (pieces seem to fly, stick to hands and clothes, fall out of bag easily, etc.) and each solution (wet hands, cup hands together, hold bag gently, etc.) to get past the obstacle. As appropriate, talk about the popcorn's fitting name.

WOW! Rhyme: *obstacle*

There's an obstacle here.
There are holes in the street.
There's an obstacle there.
There's fresh new concrete.
I can't ride my bike or skate here
    or there.
There are obstacles, obstacles
    everywhere!

Here's What It Means

verb: to understand

Synonyms—*They have nearly the same meaning.*

be aware of	sense
comprehend	take notice of
feel	think
grasp	understand

Figuratively Speaking

get it; get the picture; get your head around; get a handle on; take in; see the light

Forms of *perceive* to Share with 6s

misperception (noun)
perception (noun)
perceived (verb)
perceives (verb)
perceiving (verb)

Talk & Share

1. I didn't perceive it the same way you did.

2. Let's check our perceptions before you claim we disagree.

3. I need to get my head around how you're perceiving what I said.

4. My perception is that you are upset with me.

5. His perception that I was angry was dead wrong.

6. My mom and I perceived things differently last night.

7. My perception of the accident is that Jimmie bumped into you.

8. He has a misperception of what happened.

9. Dad perceives it as being my fault.

10. The dog perceives that there is a squirrel in the tree.

Focusing Talk: Considering Perceptions

Read "A Ruff Day" (see Resources, page 180). Discuss why the listener might form a perception that changes as more details are known. Share a time you misperceived a situation, such as feeling angry with a family member about trash on the driveway but learning more details and deciding a raccoon had been the culprit. Help children discuss similar experiences. Encourage children to be on the lookout for misperceptions.

Hands-On: Dramatizing Perceptions and Misperceptions

Invite partners to dramatize a positive and a negative way to perceive a given situation. Offer partners a choice of situations, such as the following: you get on the bus or enter the lunchroom and no one invites you to sit with them; your parent doesn't answer when you ask a question; you see your best friend playing with someone else; or your friend never calls you on the phone. Discuss children's feelings about each detail along the way.

WOW! Rhyme: **perceive**

Here's my perception
of our fight last night.
I perceive it like this:
You're wrong.
And I'm right.

Here's What It Means

adverb: every so often

Synonyms—*They have nearly the same meaning.*

in cycles   occasionally
now and again   off and on
now and then   repeatedly

Forms of *periodically* to Share with 6s

period (noun)
periodic (adjective)
periodical (noun)

Talk & Share

1. I dress up periodically.

2. I go to my cousin's house periodically.

3. I go through periods when I like to play video games.

4. We have periodic check-ups to see how we're doing.

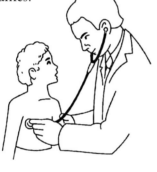

5. Magazines are called periodicals because they are usually published again and again.

6. I checked the mail periodically today.

7. I feel sleepy at the same period of time each day.

8. It helps to keep the bathroom fresh if we do a periodic cleaning.

9. I do that task periodically so I don't get behind.

10. I like to read for a period each day.

Focusing Talk:
Enjoying Activities Periodically

Model using *periodically* in a sentence as you talk about an activity you enjoy now and then. Point out that you don't do the activity all the time. Then invite children to follow your model to name activities they like to do periodically. List children's ideas. Help children make a tally chart of their ideas by category, such as whether the activity is enjoyed alone or with others, at home or in other places, and how often it's listed, and so on.

Hands-On:
Studying Periodicals

Invite children to use the word *periodical* interchangeably with magazine as they search old periodicals to locate words (or alphabet letters) which appear periodically in a particular color. Repeat the activity to locate pictures or shapes that appear periodically in any one periodical. At other times, extend exploration of periodicals to find out how often each periodical is published or how often periodicals include the same heading or topic.

WOW! Rhyme: **periodically**

Periodically, yes.
I'd say it is so.
Now and then I say, "Yes."
Now and then I say, "No."

Here's What It Means

adjective: feeling upset

Synonyms—*They have nearly the same meaning.*

angered
troubled
annoyed

Figuratively Speaking

flustered; shook up; fired up; bugged; hassled

Forms of *perturbed* to Share with 6s

perturb (verb)
perturbing (adjective, verb)
perturbs (verb)
unperturbed (adjective)

Talk & Share

1. It perturbs me when people act rude.

2. Dainty Dinosaur feels sad and then perturbed while looking at the photos.

3. It would certainly perturb me if my bike were missing.

4. Sally feels perturbed when the Cat in the Hat laughs about playing tricks.

5. I was actually unperturbed when we couldn't do what we'd planned.

6. It is perturbing to be the last one who's chosen.

7. Her words were perturbing me, so I stopped listening.

8. It perturbed me when our baby went into my room and messed it up.

9. Please don't feel perturbed if my great-grandpa doesn't hear you.

10. So what perturbs you the most about this situation?

Focusing Talk: Feeling Perturbed

As appropriate, invite help in reading aloud *The Cat in the Hat Comes Back* and/or *You Have a Friend, Dainty Dinosaur* (see Resources, page 173). Ask if Sally or Dainty Dinosaur might be feeling perturbed and why or why not. Invite children to share times when they have felt perturbed, how they acted, if their troubled feelings were resolved, and why or why not. Ask for other ideas that may have helped ease each story character's feelings.

Hands-On: Learning about Perturbing Situations

Share "It's Not My Fault!" (see Resources, page 178). Talk about why it's helpful to know which things perturb us, as well as to know which things perturb family members and friends. Provide four 3-inch-by-5-inch index cards for each child. Have children survey themselves and three family members or friends to list a couple of things that perturb each person. Have children ask family members, as needed, to help write words.

WOW! Rhyme: **perturbed**

It's perturbing
and disturbing.
I'm annoyed.
I'm so upset!

I'm perturbed.
I left my bike outside.
And now—
my bike's all wet.

Here's What It Means

verb: to think about

Synonyms—*They have nearly the same meaning.*

consider
weigh in on

Figuratively Speaking

mull over

Forms of *ponder* to Share with 6s

pondered (verb)
pondering (verb)
ponders (verb)

Talk & Share

1. Let's ponder whether we want to go or not.

2. I seem to ponder things as I'm falling asleep.

3. He sometimes ponders things so much that he then worries.

4. I pondered which sandwich I wanted.

5. Dad asked me to ponder which gift I'd like most.

6. I am pondering how the dog got out.

7. I pondered things I can do when I feel bored.

8. I pondered all the poems before I chose this one.

9. Rodin's statue of *The Thinker* represents a man who's pondering things.

10. Come ponder the possibilities with me.

Focusing Talk: Pondering Places to Go

Invite children to ponder and name places they like to visit in their home area, inside their homes, and far from where they live. List all ideas under headings, such as "Near Home," "At Home," and "Far from Home." Invite discussion about how children might travel to each place they like to visit. Then ask children to ponder which modes of transportation might require more or less money and more or less energy.

Hands-On: Appreciating One Who Seems to Ponder

Provide partners a photocopied picture of Auguste Rodin's sculpture *The Thinker*. Share "The Thinker" (see Resources, page 181). Ask children to ponder what they think the man in the sculpture is pondering. Then have partners take turns dramatizing the roles of The Thinker and someone who asks questions to learn what The Thinker is pondering. Ask volunteers to impersonate Rodin to tell what he may have pondered while sculpting.

WOW! Rhyme: *ponder*

This ponderer thinks
and ponders some more
in hopes of finding a way
to do whatever it is that I'm pondering
I'd like to be doing today.

Here's What It Means

adjective: not wanting to do something

Synonyms—*They have nearly the same meaning.*

hesitant   unenthusiastic
not eager   unwilling
shy

Forms of *reluctant* to Share with 6s

reluctance (noun)
reluctantly (adverb)

Talk & Share

1. I was reluctant to jump into the cold pool.

2. I feel reluctant about raising my hand to answer.

3. Josh noticed my reluctance to share my new game.

4. I could tell Tatum was reluctant to touch my frog.

5. Some people recycle reluctantly because it's extra work.

6. Did you notice Justine's reluctance to line up?

7. Reluctantly, I got into bed.

8. Some mornings, my little sister is reluctant to wake up.

9. My dog shows his reluctance to go outside in the rain.

10. I played reluctantly until I won my first game.

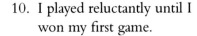

Focusing Talk:
Feeling Reluctance

Share *The Cat in the Hat* (see Resources, page 173). Ask children, "How do you think the boy and girl feel when Cat invites them to play? What would you do when Mother comes home?" Encourage children to reply, "I'd feel reluctant…," instead of "I wouldn't want to…." Help children name other situations where they might feel reluctant. Talk about times when it's wise to be reluctant until being sure an activity is safe or okay to do.

Hands-On:
Making Puppets Show Reluctance

Help children glue buttons as eyes and pre-cut yarn strands as hair onto a sock. Invite use of permanent markers to draw lips, nose, and perhaps dimples or freckles. Ask children to have their puppets show reluctance (scrunch mouth, hide eyes, look away or downward, hide behind someone, shake head, etc.) while dramatizing a story, such as *The Cat in the Hat, When Mindy Saved Hanukkah,* or *The Reluctant Dragon* (see Resources, pages 173–174).

WOW! Rhyme: **reluctant**

When I met you
and you met me,
at first,
we talked
reluctantly.

spontaneous (spon TAA nee uhs)

Here's What It Means

adjective: without being planned

Synonyms—*They have nearly the same meaning.*

not expected   not knowingly caused

not forced   suddenly

Figuratively Speaking

in the spur of the moment; off the top of my head

Forms of *spontaneous* to Share with 6s

spontaneity (noun)

spontaneously (adverb)

Talk & Share

1. We heard a spontaneous cheer from the stands.

2. I was expecting some spontaneity, but I was still totally surprised.

3. The baby giggled spontaneously.

4. The actors spontaneously bowed to the applause.

5. The curtain opened spontaneously.

6. My friends surprised me when they clapped with such spontaneity.

7. Water gushed spontaneously from the rooftop.

8. My grandma is spontaneous with her hugs.

9. She says her hugs show her spontaneous love for me.

10. We're expecting spontaneous approval.

Focusing Talk:
Considering Spontaneous Actions

Tell about a time when you acted spontaneously and later wished you had been more thoughtful before acting or speaking. An example might be telling someone "Yes" and later wishing you'd said "No" or vice versa. Help children compare spontaneous actions (crossing a street or grabbing a coat without looking) that may have consequences, to actions (picnic, phone call, visit with a friend, book or food choice) that turn out great.

Hands-On:
Celebrating Spontaneously

Talk about how birthday and holiday celebrations are generally planned in advance, rather than being celebrated spontaneously. Encourage thoughts about spontaneous ways to celebrate ordinary occasions, such as a friendly offer to help or someone saying "Thank you!" or "Good morning!" Invite small groups to pantomime spontaneous celebrations as others try to name the occasion and how it is being celebrated.

WOW! Rhyme: ***spontaneous***

I might have said, "No"

or spontaneously, "Yes."

So what did I say?

A spontaneous guess.

Here's What It Means

verb: to call forth

Synonyms—*They have nearly the same meaning.*

call out   request
invite   signal
order

Forms of *summon* to Share with 6s

summoned (verb)
summoning (verb)
summons (noun, verb)

Talk & Share

1. My friend summoned me to carry tons of books.

2. I think I should summon help.

3. Please don't summon me during rest time.

4. My alarm clock summons me to start each day!

5. I was summoned to come here immediately.

6. Uncle Paul will summon us when the pizza's ready.

7. Is Planet Earth summoning us to recycle?

8. A phone call summoned Mom to return to her office.

9. My aunt was speeding and received a summons to appear in court.

10. No one wants to get summoned to the principal's office.

Focusing Talk:
Summoning Help

Ask children when and why someone might summon help. Help children name tasks they might like to do but would need to summon help because the task requires more knowledge or more helpful hands. Talk about how and why some people might or might not like to be summoned. Invite children to share times when they did or didn't mind being summoned. Discuss polite words that can be helpful when summoning others.

Hands-On:
Writing Notes to Summon

Help children compile a list of words they might use to summon someone for help, to come to play, to ask a question, or to join them in an activity. Provide 3-inch-by-5-inch index cards and invite children to write at least one note each day in school and one note each day at home, in lieu of orally summoning their friends or family members. Remind children to utilize their lists of words and add to their lists as they write effective notes that summon.

WOW! Rhyme: *summon*

I'm summoned
and summoned
and summoned all day.
Won't somebody tell them
it's my time to play!

thrifty (THRIF tee)

Here's What It Means

adjective: careful use of something, like money

Synonyms—*They have nearly the same meaning.*

not wasting
saving

Figuratively Speaking

making ends meet; penny-pinching;
cutting corners

Forms of *thrifty* to Share with 6s

thrift (noun, adjective)
thriftier (adjective)
thriftiest (adjective)

Talk & Share

1. We need to be thrifty with our planet's water supply.

2. My sister is thriftier than I am when we go shopping.

3. I'm being thrifty this week so I'll have more next week.

4. Grandpa is the thriftiest person in my family.

5. Uncle Pey says it's good to practice thrift.

6. Mom says we could all be thriftier.

7. I am thrifty with paper towels.

8. A new thrift store opened in our neighborhood.

9. Thrifty spending helps put money away for a rainy day.

10. I am trying to be thriftier with paper now.

 Focusing Talk:
Being Thrifty Citizens

Help children name areas where being thrifty is helpful to themselves, to others, and to our planet as a whole. Ideas may include saving water, paper, money, electricity, recycling various materials, and so on. Encourage children to expand ideas, such as how saving paper saves trees, turning off lights saves electricity, taking short showers saves water, or saving money helps one be prepared for an unexpected or spontaneous emergency.

Hands-On:
Making "Thrifty Art"

Share "Earth Says" (see Resources, page 177). Provide glue, markers, and various reusable items, such as cardboard rolls from paper towels and tissue, scrap paper, egg cartons, water bottle caps, plastic tubs and lids, and used string and twist ties. Invite partners or small groups to create "Thrifty Art" masterpieces. Encourage children to make signs to name each piece of art and have each creator, or artisan, autograph work.

WOW! Rhyme: **thrifty**

I'm thrifty, thrifty, thrifty.
I'm as thrifty as can be.
I'm saving water,
saving dimes,
and saving energy.

Here's What It Means

adjective: empty

Synonyms—*They have nearly the same meaning.*

empty
not filled up
unused

Figuratively Speaking

gone; out to lunch; nobody home

Forms of *vacant* to Share with 6s

vacancies (noun)
vacancy (noun)

Talk & Share

1. We can play ball on the vacant lot.
2. There's a vacancy at the motel.
3. Our apartment building has some vacancies.
4. Right now, there's a vacant spot on our team.
5. I think that vacant house feels haunted.
6. Maybe there will be some vacancies tomorrow.
7. The cat may be sleeping in a vacant house somewhere.
8. Our house will be vacant when we go on vacation.
9. There's some vacant space here in my desk.
10. One side of our garage is always vacant.

Focusing Talk:
Thinking about Vacancies

Help children name reasons why there might be lots of vacancies in a motel (no signage out front to guide guests, motel is not clean, it's out of the way so people might not go by it, it's not listed in travel books, no one knows about it, a "No Vacancies" sign is always out so people think there are no vacancies, etc.). At another time, help children consider why there might not be vacancies for teachers or students in a particular school.

Hands-On:
Making Vacancy Signage

Provide paper, markers, and double-faced tape. Have children write *Vacancy* on one side of their paper and *No Vacancy* on the other side. Invite children to post their signs on their seats to denote a vacancy when they are away and no vacancy when they are in their seats, or when they'd like to reserve the seat. Children will enjoy making duplicate "Vacancy"/"No Vacancy" signs to attach to bedroom or bathroom doors at home.

WOW! Rhyme: *vacant*

On our vacant lot,
there's not much there.
No building.
No house.
Just dirt and air.

Here's What It Means

verb: to give up or to produce

Synonyms—*They have nearly the same meaning.*

blossom   give way
earn   make
give   wait

Figuratively Speaking

give it up

Forms of *yield* to Share with 6s

yielded (verb)
yielding (verb)
yields (verb)

Talk & Share

1. The sign tells us to yield and let that car go first.

2. The cookie recipe yields five dozen cookies.

3. I am yielding to let you talk.

4. This tree yields delicious oranges.

5. I have found that studying yields good grades.

6. My uncle says his job yields little pay.

7. Our berry-picking day yielded five quarts of berries.

8. Buster might be yielding to Kym in their arm-wrestling challenge.

9. On the way to school, we pass signs that tell us to stop and to yield.

10. Cars have to yield the right-of-way at the corner by our apartment building.

Focusing Talk:
Yielding the Floor

Children will enjoy learning the idiom "to yield the floor" as they take turns telling about times they stood aside to let another person go ahead. For a time, encourage children to indicate they are finished talking by saying, "I yield the floor." Invite the talker in a group to hold a "talking stick" to designate how the talker gets to talk as others yield the floor to be listeners. Encourage use of a talking stick in groups to gently discourage interruptions.

Hands-On:
Making Yield Signs

Invite children to ask family members to help them find four yield signs in their community. Encourage children to use a finger to trace around a yield sign and note the sign's shape as a triangle that points downward. Help children use yellow paper and black markers to make yield signs they can place in appropriate places in the classroom or at home. You might also have children hold up yield signs when "yielding the floor."

WOW! Rhyme: *yield*

I'll yield the floor to you, I will.
And you might think you'll walk.
But that's not right.
This kind of yielding
gives you a turn to talk.

AGE 7

- [ ] accessible
- [ ] accumulate
- [ ] aghast
- [ ] alternative
- [ ] colossal
- [ ] competent
- [ ] consecutive
- [ ] diligent
- [ ] divulge
- [ ] effective
- [ ] empathize
- [ ] exceedingly
- [ ] expedite
- [ ] indicate
- [ ] intimidate
- [ ] manipulate
- [ ] nonchalant
- [ ] ominous

- [ ] personable
- [ ] perspective
- [ ] pertinent
- [ ] priority
- [ ] prolific
- [ ] prone
- [ ] regret
- [ ] reminisce
- [ ] replenish
- [ ] simultaneous
- [ ] sustain
- [ ] tedious
- [ ] tradition
- [ ] tranquil
- [ ] transparent
- [ ] treacherous
- [ ] verify
- [ ] vigor

accessible (ak SES uh buhl)

Here's What It Means

adjective: can be entered

Synonyms—*They have nearly the same meaning.*

can get into   reachable
not blocked   within reach
passable

Forms of *accessible* to Share with 7s

access (noun, verb)
accessed (verb)
accessibility (noun)
inaccessible (adjective)

Talk & Share

1. My classroom is accessible from the side door.

2. The house hasn't been accessed because the door is locked.

3. The top of Mount McKinley is not easily accessible.

4. My teacher says my goal to finish this book is accessible.

5. Children have access to movies that are rated G.

6. Joey's ball went down the sewer and is now inaccessible.

7. The store announced a date for the new toy's accessibility.

8. I wish my grandparents had access to the Internet and e-mail.

9. The pool is accessible for anyone to swim after 3:00 each day.

10. Someone needs to limit my brother's accessibility to my room!

Focusing Talk:
Discussing Accessibility of Characters

Share "Rapunzel" or *Tikki Tikki Tembo* (see Resources, pages 173–174). As appropriate, stop to ask children why the story's character is trapped, or not able to access a way out. Encourage children's responses in sentences using *accessible* and its forms. Similarly, invite children to predict ways the character might gain greater accessibility. Resume reading and have children use sentences to check on and report their predictions.

Hands-On:
Blocking Access

Have children hold hands in a circle to play "Cat and Rat." One child, Cat, goes around the outside of the circle while Rat is inside. On a signal, Cat moves to tag Rat as children raise and lower their joined hands to block Cat's access. If Cat gains access to the inner circle, then children try to lock Cat inside, helping to protect Rat or to help Rat be inaccessible. When Cat tags Rat, both characters choose classmates to take their places.

WOW! Rhyme: **accessible**

This was once an accessible place.

But now—inaccessible space.

Too high in the air.

No ladder;

no stair.

No way we can access that vase!

---

accumulate (uh KYUUM yuu laat)

Here's What It Means

verb: to collect over time

Synonyms—*They have nearly the same meaning.*

acquire   gather
assemble   pile up
build up

Forms of *accumulate* to Share with 7s

accumulated (verb)
accumulates (verb)
accumulating (verb)
accumulation (noun)

Talk & Share

1. Storm clouds accumulated all through the night.

2. I've been accumulating baseball cards for years now.

3. We can make a snowman with the snow we've accumulated.

4. Scientists accumulated information proving that Pluto is not a planet.

5. We get a reward when our class accumulates twenty points.

6. My little brother is accumulating too many dinosaur toys.

7. An accumulation of evidence proved the accused was guilty.

8. I need to accumulate two more books to have the whole series.

9. We are accumulating a ton of newspapers in our recycling bin.

10. Let's protect our planet from an accumulation of pollutants.

Focusing Talk:
Noticing Accumulations

Tell children about a personal accumulation, such as recipes, ticket stubs, books, glassware, antiques, sports memorabilia, newspapers, or friends who share an interest. Invite children to use *accumulate* and its forms to share times they have accumulated items. Talk about accumulations, such as snow, rain, dust, leaves, bug bites, or fingerprints, which can present beauty, offer nourishment, cause discomfort, or help with work.

Hands-On:
Tending Accumulated Sprouts

Ask children to bring in an old sock and wear it over one shoe during a walk through a grassy area. After the walk, have children carefully remove the sock and, using a magnifying glass or loupe, observe how and what the sock has accumulated during its time on the grass. Help children place each sock in a foil-lined box covered by 1 inch of soil. Have children water and observe accumulative sprouting over the following weeks.

WOW! Rhyme: *accumulate*

Accumulate books,
Accumulate A's,
Accumulate rocks, if you must.
Accumulate cards,
or other such things,
but please don't accumulate dust!

Here's What It Means

adjective: feeling horrified

Synonyms—*They have nearly the same meaning.*

distressed   shocked
flabbergasted   stunned
offended   upset

Talk & Share

1. Dad was aghast at the price of the car repair.

2. My teacher was aghast to see our messy classroom.

3. The climber stared, aghast at the steepness of the mountain.

4. I was aghast when I saw how much snow I had to remove.

5. Grandma was aghast when my brother spoke so rudely.

6. My classmates were aghast at the long list of extinct animals.

7. We were aghast when our model airplane crashed.

8. I was aghast when Brayden beat me in the race.

9. Visitors looked aghast as they left the spook house.

10. The man appeared aghast that his pants had ripped.

Focusing Talk: Feeling Aghast

Model an aghast expression (wide eyes, open mouth, eyebrows up) before sharing a time when you felt aghast. Read aloud a poem, such as "Friendly Frederick Fuddlestone," "True Story" (see Resources, page 174), or "My True Story," (page 179). Discuss why each character or narrator had an apparent feeling of being aghast. Invite children to make aghast expressions as you reread a poem. Have children share, "I'd feel/I felt aghast when… " to tell of experiences or thoughts.

Hands-On: Causing Aghast Expressions

Provide 8½-inch-by-11-inch cardstock and a tongue depressor for each child to make a two-sided mask. Help children mark and cut out eye holes or a rectangular window for eyes. Have children draw a horrifying face on one side of the cardstock and a face that looks aghast on the other side. Tell children to tape the tongue depressor to the bottom of their mask. Invite children to use their masks to prompt someone to look Aghast or to look aghast at another's mask.

WOW! Rhyme: **aghast**

I'm telling you I feel aghast.
I was shocked when I saw you fly past.
I was peddling full blast.
Then I saw you soar past.
And now, I am last… and aghast!

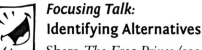 **alternative** (awl TUR nuh tiv)

Here's What It Means

noun: choice between two or more possibilities
adjective: other; different

Synonyms—*They have nearly the same meaning.*

choice   selection
option   substitute
possibility

Figuratively Speaking

fork in the road

Talk & Share

1. Some Native Americans had no alternative but to move to Oklahoma.

2. Many people don't drive cars and use alternative ways to get to work.

3. Dad listens to an alternative radio station to hear rock music.

4. Talking about a disagreement is an alternative to fighting.

5. What are alternatives to ordering a baked potato?

6. Mom selected the alternative meat for herself at dinner.

7. Can you find an alternative way to solve that math problem?

8. One alternative to using a plastic bag is to carry a cloth bag.

9. Automobile makers are building cars that use alternative fuels.

10. This map offers three alternative routes.

Focusing Talk: Identifying Alternatives

Share *The Frog Prince* (see Resources, page 173), pausing when a story character must make a choice. Ask children to help the story character with suggestions that begin with: "An alternative to the frog's giving the princess her ball would be… " or "An alternative to the princess's leaving the frog in the water would be.…" Read aloud "Let's Talk" (page 178), and encourage discussion about alternative ways to act during a disagreement.

Hands-On: Illustrating Alternatives

Help children draw a tree trunk on the lower half of a piece of paper and write "Alternative Ways to Act." Have children draw limbs and branches to complete their trees. Tell children to think back to the activity above as they write on each limb or branch an alternative way to act when angry. Ideas may include: talk to someone, count to ten, go jogging, or write angry words on paper to wad up and toss into the trash basket.

WOW! Rhyme: **alternative**

Left or right?

Out or in?

Weigh the alternatives.

Then—

begin.

WOW! Word **colossal** (kuh LOS uhl)

Here's What It Means

adjective: very large

Synonyms—*They have nearly the same meaning.*

enormous   immense
giant   tremendous
gigantic   vast
huge

Form of *colossal* to Share with 7s

colossus (noun)

Talk & Share

1. The presidents' heads on Mount Rushmore are colossal!

2. The colossal flood covered the treetops.

3. A colossus is a gigantic statue such as those created in ancient times.

4. I couldn't finish eating what seemed to be a colossal bowl of soup.

5. They don't make a pizza colossal enough to feed our whole family.

6. Some cars seem colossal when compared to very small cars.

7. The Colossus of Rhodes was one of the Seven Wonders of the Ancient World.

8. Avi and Julio seem to have had a colossal misunderstanding.

9. People never forget a colossal tsunami.

10. That colossal truck can't possibly fit under the bridge.

Focusing Talk:
Considering Colossal Things

Talk about the Colossus of Rhodes, one of the Seven Wonders of the Ancient World (http://www.rhodesguide.com/rhodes/colossus_rhodes.php). Ask children to tell about colossal things they have seen, such as a colossal cookie, water slide, statue, or bridge. To invite discussion of imaginary ideas, you might say, "If a hummingbird were colossal...." You might also read *The Mysterious Giant of Barletta* (see Resources, page 173).

Hands-On:
Building Colossal Structures

Provide small groups an assortment of base ten blocks, Unifix cubes, centimeter cubes, or other math manipulatives. Invite each group to build a colossal structure, such as a tower, bridge, skyscraper, and so on. Have groups secretly count and record the number of units used in their structures. Invite groups to visit all structures, register their names, and submit comments about each structure's engineering, along with guessing its total units.

WOW! Rhyme: **colossal**

A T-rex bone—
it turned to stone
on the side of a hill
for years until—
Someone found a fossil.
Wow!
Colossal!

Here's What It Means

adjective: able to do something well

Synonyms—*They have nearly the same meaning.*

able
capable
skilled

Figuratively Speaking

ready, willing, and able; in the know

Forms of *competent* to Share with 7s

competence (noun)
competencies (noun)
competency (noun)
incompetent (adjective)

Talk & Share

1. Our coach is a competent soccer player.

2. Dontae thinks he's incompetent in math.

3. My teacher says I'm a competent piano player.

4. My dad likes to test my competence in geography.

5. Next month we'll be tested for competency in reading and math.

6. Mom's friend is a competent sculptress.

7. Do you have special competencies in the graphic arts?

8. Nguyen thinks he is incompetent as a tennis player.

9. Little Mikel wants to be as competent a reader as her big sister.

10. I'll be a more competent swimmer by next summer.

Focusing Talk:
Recognizing Competencies

Help children name people they know who have special competencies. Create a T-chart with names down the left-hand column and each person's competency in the right-hand column. Model use of complete sentences and forms of *competent* as children share. For example, you might say, "My competencies are in art." Add chart pages, as needed, to include all children's names (and your own) with a competency each person claims.

Hands-On:
Feeling Pride of Competency

Provide drawing paper for children to illustrate ten competencies each child can claim. For example, math competencies may be shown with a clock, Roman numerals, or a fractions problem. Remind children to include all kinds of skills, such as bike riding or sandwich making, in which they feel competent. Encourage children to include a caption for each picture, share with the group, and then take home to share with family members.

WOW! Rhyme: **competent**

I'm competent in math
and a competent reader.
I'm also a competent swimmer and
     leader.
It's fun to be competent,
but sometimes,
I'm not.
And that's when I try
to just give my best shot.

Here's What It Means

adjective: in order without any interruption

Synonyms—*They have nearly the same meaning.*

continuous
following closely
sequence

Form of *consecutive* to Share with 7s

consecutively (adverb)

Talk & Share

1. My bus has been early three days consecutively.

2. The teacher returned our papers by last names and in consecutive order.

3. My skateboarding trick has improved with each consecutive attempt.

4. Though they did not serve consecutively, two presidents were named George Bush.

5. June and July are consecutive months.

6. One day during "Shark Week" on the Discovery Channel, I watched four consecutive shark shows.

7. Our team lost many games consecutively before a big winning streak.

8. For many consecutive weeks, we've had Sunday dinner at Grandma's.

9. On my street, five consecutive houses are painted gray.

10. The mail carrier makes deliveries at consecutive houses where possible.

Focusing Talk:
Noticing Consecutive Order

Talk about common uses of consecutive ordering, such as lists arranged alphabetically, numerically, or by color, size, and so on. Have children line up in consecutive order by the first letter of their first or last names, and then reorder consecutively by birthdays, color of eyes or shoes, or by age in months. Invite children to name more uses of consecutive order, such as calendar months, days of the week, or books shelved by author or last name.

Hands-On:
Identifying Consecutive Patterns

Provide copies of three sample patterns—such as BBBCBBBCBBBC, 497649764976, or $¢$¢$¢—for children to identify each consecutively repeated pattern. Then ask partners to create more patterns that show repeating consecutive elements. Have partners exchange papers with another pair to identify each other's patterns. You may want to help partners create incomplete patterns for other pairs to identify and complete.

WOW! Rhyme: ***consecutive***

1, 2, 3.
Do, re, mi.
Consecutive order
is easy for me.

Here's What It Means

adjective: hard-working

Synonyms—*They have nearly the same meaning.*

careful   persistent
conscientious   studious
not a quitter   undiscouraged

Forms of *diligent* to Share with 7s

diligence (noun)
diligently (adverb)

Talk & Share

1. I have been diligent in searching for my notebook.

2. Some diligence may help solve that difficult problem.

3. My sister worked diligently to learn how to tie her shoe.

4. Abraham Lincoln practiced diligence to win equality for all.

5. Your diligence paid off with an *A* on the spelling test.

6. Women had to be diligent in their work to gain the right to vote.

7. My brother studied diligently so he could earn his driving license.

8. Our baseball team practices diligently in hopes we can win our games.

9. Ruis was diligent and finished every chore within twenty minutes.

10. Solving a one-thousand-piece puzzle requires sheer diligence.

Focusing Talk: Discussing Diligence

Share a story, such as "The Little Red Hen" or "The Tortoise and the Hare." Engage children in conversation about a story's character or a friend who practiced diligence. Ask how one might recognize and measure diligence. Examples might include working for one day versus two weeks or looking for and then finding a lost item. Invite sharing of experiences in using and measuring diligent efforts.

Hands-On: Practicing Diligence

Provide children a list of tasks, such as the following, to be completed within the week: bounce a ball one hundred times non-stop; print full names of all family members; find the sum of all classmates' ages; locate *conscientious* in a standard or online dictionary and record its meaning; pat head and rub belly at the same time. On Friday, have children write, in their journals, a comparison of the diligence required to complete the tasks.

WOW! Rhyme: **diligent**

A diligent worker
worked diligently
to finish a job one day.
Then, diligently,
the worker cleaned up
in time to go out to play.

Here's What It Means

verb: to tell

Synonyms—*They have nearly the same meaning.*

make known
reveal

Figuratively Speaking

spill the beans; let the cat out of the bag

Forms of *divulge* to Share with 7s

divulged (verb)
divulges (verb)
divulging (verb)

Talk & Share

1. Please don't divulge our secret.

2. I can't get Mom to divulge what's in the package.

3. My teacher hasn't divulged her age to the class.

4. Harriet Tubman never divulged details about the Underground Railroad.

5. Box turtles bury their eggs without leaving any signs that would divulge the location.

6. I can't divulge where I like to hide when we play "Hide and Seek."

7. My mom never divulges her phone number to strangers.

8. Oscar overheard me divulging my unusual middle name.

9. Scientists divulged information that led them to decide Pluto was not a planet.

10. I divulged the answers as classmates graded one another's tests.

Focusing Talk: Divulging Secrets

Secretly share a one-sentence message with the first child in a line of eight or more children. Have the next child say, "Please divulge the secret!", to receive the whispered message. Continue similarly until the last child in line divulges the secret to all. Using *divulge* and its forms, help children discuss possible consequences of divulging a secret. Talk about how a message may undergo change when it's being repeated.

Hands-On: Divulging a Genre or Category

Write on chart paper the poems "Fiction" (see Resources, page 177), "Nonfiction" (page 179), and "Biography" (page 175). Read aloud and use the words *genre* and *category*; *nonfiction* and *real*; *true* and *not true*; and *make-believe* and *fantasy* to discuss each poem's ideas. Then, invite partners to research and divulge the genre of two or more classroom library books. Have children use the poems to make bookmarks that divulge each book's genre.

WOW! Rhyme: **divulge**

I'd never divulge our secret.
I'd never divulge a clue.
I'll keep all divulging details to myself.
I'm hoping that you will, too.

Here's What It Means

adjective: a result that one wants; positive outcome

Synonyms—*They have nearly the same meaning.*

capable	useful
efficient	valuable
practical	worthwhile
successful	

Forms of *effective* to Share with 7s

effect (noun)
effectively (adverb)

Talk & Share

1. Running in place is effective to keep me warm in cold weather.

2. The mechanic's repairs effectively made our car run like new.

3. Blisters were the painful effect of walking in ill-fitting shoes.

4. I think an *A* on my spelling test proves that I studied effectively.

5. The medicine will begin to work, or take effect, in thirty minutes.

6. Mom asked if I had effectively cleaned my room.

7. The Emancipation Proclamation effectively helped slaves to be free.

8. I have an effective strategy for cleaning up that spill.

9. The effect of a mixture of baking soda and water is to ease the pain of a sting.

10. A belt or suspenders can effectively hold up a pair of pants.

Focusing Talk:
Avoiding Problems Effectively

Talk about how effective strategies help to avoid problems. Create a T-chart, the left side of which lists examples of age-appropriate jobs, such as student, soccer player, choir member, or dog walker. Encourage use of *effective* and its forms to discuss, and record on the right side, effective actions, choices, or results around each job, such as getting sleep helps one be an effective student or dribbling practice results in being an effective soccer player.

Hands-On:
Solving Problems Effectively

Talk about how effective strategies can help solve problems. Present the problems 47 + __ = 78 and __ − 21 = 22. Ask children to write an effective strategy to find each missing number. Encourage all responses that work, ranging from drawing pictures to performing an opposite operation. You may want to call on children's ideas as a springboard for naming and using effective problem-solving strategies during future math lessons.

WOW! Rhyme: *effective*

What's effective?
What works great?
Effective plans
make results first-rate.

Here's What It Means

verb: to understand someone's feelings

Synonyms—*They have nearly the same meaning.*

have feeling for
hear and understand
relate to

Figuratively Speaking

tune in; dig it; get what you mean

Forms of *empathize* to Share with 7s

empathetic (adjective)
empathized (verb)
empathizes (verb)
empathizing (verb)
empathy (noun)

Talk & Share

1. I can empathize when you say you feel lost in this huge building.

2. Mom was empathetic when I didn't receive a birthday card.

3. I appreciated my friend's empathy when my arm was in a cast.

4. The coach's empathy gave us confidence to finish the game.

5. Veena's empathy helped me sort out my unhappy feelings.

6. Grandpa empathized with me, and I felt hopeful again.

7. Dad noticed I was feeling safe, and his empathy really helped.

8. Doodle was empathizing when she asked if my elbow hurt.

9. Our neighbors were empathetic when our cat was lost.

10. I am thankful when my friend empathizes with how I'm feeling.

Focusing Talk: Identifying Empathy

Read "Afraidy Day" (see Resources, page 174) and "My Faces" (page 179). Talk about how feeling afraid is one of many ways a person can feel at any time. Encourage children to tell about times they have felt the fears named in the first poem and what empathetic words from others could help them feel less afraid or more safe. Children might say, "His empathy told me he felt my fear of losing," or "I received empathy from my friend when I cried."

Hands-On: Practicing Empathy

Provide 3-inch-by-5-inch index cards for children to create a deck of "Feeling-Faces Cards" that includes happy, guilty, sad, angry, afraid, surprised, bored, and proud. Have a child draw a card and dramatize its feeling face as others give empathy, such as "You're feeling angry," "You look happy," "I'm wondering if you're bored," and so on. The receiver of empathy tells how it feels when others notice what he or she is feeling.

WOW! Rhyme: **empathize**

Today it felt good—
my mom understood.
She gave empathy once
    when she knew I was sad.
And she empathized later when I
    acted mad.

Today, it felt nice—
I got empathy twice.

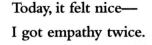

Here's What It Means

adverb: very much

Synonyms—*They have nearly the same meaning.*

amazingly   splendidly
extremely   tremendously
outstandingly   unusually
remarkably

Forms of *exceedingly* to Share with 7s

exceed (verb)
exceeds (verb)
exceeded (verb)
exceeding (verb)

Talk & Share

1. Our teacher didn't believe Jonathan's exceedingly wild excuses.

2. An exceedingly large number of fish were on display at the aquarium.

3. This year's cold weather exceeds our normal temperatures.

4. The stores were exceedingly full of holiday shoppers on Saturday.

5. I am exceedingly quiet when my dad chooses to sleep in.

6. That driver chose to exceed the speed limit.

7. Exceeding the speed limit is illegal.

8. Dry weather killed an exceedingly large number of plants in our garden.

9. Trains and railroads brought exceedingly great changes to people's lives in America.

10. We spent an exceedingly long time at the farmer's market.

Focusing Talk: Noticing Exceedingly Long or Short Words

List children's last names in a column with letters lined up under one another. Ask which names are exceedingly long or short. Then note exceedingly long and short words by plotting words, such as *I, in, and, went, write, rained,* or *hopeful,* vertically or horizontally such that the numbers from 1 to 10 are each represented by a word with that number of letters. This activity provides practice in decoding and encoding words.

Hands-On: Reading Exceedingly Slow... or Fast

Share an alliterative poem, such as "Charlie's Chickens" or "She Sells Sea Shells" (see Resources, pages 182) that offer practice in phonemic awareness, phonics, and reading with fluency. Ask volunteers to read a poem slowly or exceedingly fast. Talk about how a tongue twister twists the tongue only if it's read exceedingly fast. Invite partners to race a clock to twist their tongues reading familiar poems exceedingly fast.

WOW! Rhyme: *exceedingly*

My parents stood looking aghast
when my tongue flew exceedingly fast:
"I passed! I am cast!
I'm cast! I passed!
I passed! I passed!
I'm cast! I'm cast!"
I talked so exceedingly fast.
My words, they went flying right past.

"Uh... why are you looking aghast?"
  I asked.

Here's What It Means

verb: to hurry up

Synonyms—*They have nearly the same meaning.*

quicken
speed up
to go faster

Figuratively Speaking

get with it; get a move on; full speed ahead

Forms of *expedite* to Share with 7s

expedited (verb, adjective)
expedites (verb)
expediting (verb)
expeditious (adjective)
expeditiously (adverb)

Talk & Share

1. We may need to expedite things and travel sooner than we'd planned.

2. The new traffic light expedites the flow of traffic through here.

3. Stores tend to expedite the celebration of holidays.

4. Packages go by air if customers pay for expedited service.

5. Grandpop expedited my gift so it would arrive on time.

6. Hearing your voice makes me want to expedite my trip to see you.

7. Let's see if we can move everything expeditiously to the hall.

8. I expedited my book report to meet its due date.

9. My friend is expediting an invitation to me.

10. Our movers were more expeditious than Grandma expected.

Focusing Talk: Traveling Expeditiously

Talk about why people may sometimes need to expedite themselves or things, such as a letter, money, household belongings, machinery parts, foods, and so on, from one place to another. Create a T-chart, listing down the left side ideas to be expedited. Enlist ideas about why each idea might need to be expedited. Help children list in the chart's right column ways each idea could be expeditiously moved from one place to the other.

Hands-On: Expediting a Task

Provide scissors and reusable sheets of 8½-inch-by-11-inch paper. Have partners work to find the most expeditious way to cut a sheet of paper into two pieces exactly the same size (fold in half and cut on the line). Then challenge children to experiment to find the most expeditious way to cut a sheet into equal parts where each piece is a fourth, third, sixth, ninth, or tenth of the whole. Have partners report their discoveries to the group.

WOW! Rhyme: **expedite**

This package must be expedited.
It's gotta get there fast!
Expedite it!
Expedite it!
Ice cream will not last!

Here's What It Means

verb: to point out or show

Synonyms—*They have nearly the same meaning.*

give a sign
reveal
tell

Forms of *indicate* to Share with 7s

indicated (verb)
indicates (verb)
indicating (verb)
indication (noun)
indicative (adjective)
indicator (noun)

Talk & Share

1. His low grades indicate his lack of understanding.

2. The footprints by the garbage indicated raccoons had been here.

3. Her stomach ache is indicative of eating too much candy.

4. Dad's collection of books is one indication that he enjoys reading.

5. Holes in the backyard could indicate a dog who likes to dig.

6. My sister's silence indicates a possibility that she's angry with me.

7. Mud on Grandma's knees is an indicator that she's been gardening.

8. Saving for a camera indicates my interest in photography.

9. His accent is an indication that he may be from Mexico.

10. A thumbs-up is one way of indicating approval.

Focusing Talk: Noting Indicators

Ask children to observe your behavior and look for clues that may indicate your thoughts. Help children name indicators as you walk toward the door, stop and point a finger to your forehead, and turn and head in another direction. Invite children to use forms of *indicate* in sentences to tell about other behaviors they observe, such as that someone going toward a pencil sharpener or water fountain is likely planning to sharpen a pencil or is thirsty.

Hands-On: Gaining Information from Indicators

Remind children that we often gain information from indicators. Provide ten 3-inch-by-5-inch index cards for partners to create "Indicator" cards. Have children draw or cut and paste pictures to indicate ideas, such as a person is cold (shivering or holding onto a coat); tiredness (person yawning); go this way (arrow); person has runny nose (holding box of tissues); location of sun (plant leaning); and so on. Have children use cards to challenge friends.

WOW! Rhyme: *indicate*

There's a needle with the nurse—
Might that indicate the nurse
wants to see me to converse
or might she be planning worse?
Oh! That needle with the nurse
indicates a *whole* lot worse!
Uh, it indicates the nurse
isn't planning to converse.
Yes! That needle with
  the nurse
means it's time to hit reverse!

Here's What It Means

verb: to make afraid

Synonyms—*They have nearly the same meaning.*

bully	scare
frighten	terrorize
harass	threaten

Forms of *intimidate* to Share with 7s

intimidated (verb, adjective)

intimidates (verb)

intimidating (verb, adjective)

intimidation (noun)

intimidator (noun)

Talk & Share

1. Bobby intimidates everyone on the playground.

2. My sister tries to use intimidation to get me to do her chores.

3. I used to be intimidated by chapter books, but I read them now.

4. My neighbor's dog intimidates me when it barks.

5. A mile seems like an intimidating distance to run.

6. Julianna intimidated my friend with what she thought was teasing.

7. Lewis and Clark were not intimidated by their long and difficult exploration.

8. Right now, the idea of moving to a new school is intimidating me.

9. I keep walking and ignore intimidators.

10. I don't let a book's big words intimidate me.

Focusing Talk:
Discussing Intimidation

Introduce the topic of bullying and feeling intimidation by reading the book, *The Recess Queen* (see Resources, page 173), or poem, "Bulldog Bully" (page 176). Ask children to identify the intimidators in each selection and how each character intimidated another character. You might share personal experiences to encourage an open discussion of feelings around times when someone has intimidated another person or been the victim of intimidation.

Hands-On:
Naming the Intimidator and Intimidated

Have children draw a line down the middle of a 4-inch-by-6-inch index card for two 4-inch-by-3-inch halves. Ask children to do research to name two animals, such as cat and mouse, who are natural enemies. Invite children to draw or cut and paste one animal's picture on each half of the card. Collate cards and, with the clock as the intimidator, ask each child to draw a card and use forms of *intimidate* to describe, within thirty seconds, the animals' relationship.

WOW! Rhyme: *intimidate*

Let's discuss intimidation.

Here's a bit of information:

One who tries intimidation

oughta try out imitation.

How's it feel—intimidation?

Should *that* boss go on vacation?

Here's What It Means

verb: to control something for a good or bad result

Synonyms—*They have nearly the same meaning.*

guide   operate
handle   trick
influence   use
manage

Forms of *manipulate* to Share with 7s

manipulated (verb)
manipulates (verb)
manipulating (verb)
manipulation (noun)
manipulative (adjective)
manipulator (noun)

Talk & Share

1. Sculptors manipulate clay to form all sorts of shapes.

2. The two-year-old manipulated the knobs on the toy.

3. I like to help Grandma manipulate the dough when she bakes bread.

4. The construction worker is manipulating levers to operate the forklift.

5. My baby brother is a manipulator when he cries to get Mom's attention.

6. Playing the piano requires good finger manipulation.

7. My neighbor is so manipulative that I end up playing whatever she wants.

8. I saw John try to manipulate the pencil sharpener, but it still didn't work.

9. Manuel manipulated his bike to do all sorts of wheelies.

10. I don't trust someone who manipulates people.

Focusing Talk: Talking Manipulation

Say, "Two, four, six, eight. How might you manipulate?" Help children use forms of *manipulate* to tell about manipulating numbers to reach another number. For example, ways to reach 58 might include "17 + 22 + 19," "58 − 0," "263 − 205," and so on. Add challenge to include other math operations. At another time, discuss how it feels to be manipulated or to be the manipulator. Help children talk about their feelings from both perspectives.

Hands-On: Manipulating Objects

Show children the site http://www.lineridergames.net/; here they can draw roadways and manipulate a vehicle without crashing it. Using common sense and trial-and-error manipulations, children learn about gravity, friction, angles, and physics—for every action there is an equal and opposite reaction. At another time, help children manipulate paper to create airplanes, folding corners up or down to change an airplane's flight.

WOW! Rhyme: *manipulate*

Two, four, six, eight—
How might I manipulate?
A switch or lever lights a light.
Words and actions stop a fight.
Two, four, six, eight—
How might I manipulate?

nonchalant (non shuh LONT)

Here's What It Means

adjective: casual

Synonyms—*They have nearly the same meaning.*

calm   not caring
carefree   not concerned
cool   unstressed
mellow

Figuratively Speaking

easygoing; laid back; take in stride

Forms of *nonchalant* to Share with 7s

nonchalance (noun)
nonchalantly (adverb)

Talk & Share

1. She seemed nonchalant about the bloody cut on her hand.

2. Our cat pranced nonchalantly across the dining room table.

3. Quite nonchalantly, my teacher announced a pop quiz.

4. The president can never be nonchalant about such an important job.

5. The bully nonchalantly cut in line.

6. Dad asked nonchalantly if we wanted a puppy.

7. He walked into the room with confidence and nonchalance.

8. Justin does math with such nonchalance that he makes it look easy.

9. My friend is nonchalant about her famous relative.

10. Mom walked in as I was wrapping her gift, so I nonchalantly hid it.

Focusing Talk:
Discussing Nonchalance

Introduce the concept of feeling and/or acting nonchalant by reading *Pierre: A Cautionary Tale in Five Chapters and a Prologue* or *The Story of Ferdinand* (see Resources, page 173). Talk about how and why the main character shows nonchalance. Share a time when you felt nonchalant and why. Invite children to similarly share times when they have felt nonchalant, such as when a job is well done so there's no need to worry.

Hands-On:
Comparing Nonchalance with Excitement

Help partners use chenille sticks to create the words *yes* and *no* and glue each word onto its own sheet of heavy paper. Have each child write a list of four yes-no questions, two of which would be exciting for the partner to answer, such as "Would you like a new puppy?" and two rather ho-hum questions, such as "Might it rain today?" Have partners take turns asking and answering questions with excitement or with total nonchalance.

WOW! Rhyme: **nonchalant**

He doesn't fret.
He doesn't worry.
He's never, ever in a hurry.
Nothing
does he ever want.
His attitude
is nonchalant.

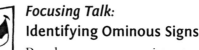
Here's What It Means

adjective: a sign of something bad to come

Synonyms—*They have nearly the same meaning.*

alarming   threatening
frightening   unlucky
scary

Form of *ominous* to Share with 7s

ominously (adverb)

Talk & Share

1. The ominous black cloud had us preparing for an approaching storm.

2. The villain laughed ominously.

3. I hid under my covers at the ominous sound of footsteps in the hall.

4. Mrs. Onie turned pale when she heard the ominous news.

5. The ominous weather report made us fear that the hurricane would hit our area hard.

6. Mom spoke ominously as I started to toss my coat on the floor.

7. During our campout, we heard an ominous sound in the dark woods.

8. Her ominous warning had us all on our best behavior.

9. The volcano gave an ominous rumble.

10. An ominous sound in the jungle may warn smaller animals.

 Focusing Talk:
Identifying Ominous Signs

Read an age-appropriate story, such as a tale from *In a Dark, Dark Room and Other Scary Stories* or *Scary Stories to Read When It's Dark* (see Resources, page 173). Help children identify the ominous idea in a story and support their opinions. Help children name other kinds of ominous scenarios, such as a dog's growling, a tree's browning leaves, or a watch that loses time. Record children's ideas and reasoning.

Hands-On:
Writing and Publishing Ominous Tales

Remind children that to say that something is ominous is to predict a not-so-pleasant happening. Invite children to use their list from above as a problem-solution pattern to tell and write a story narrative. Although children will likely begin with the ominous idea and conclude with a solution, encourage beginning with a solution and ending with the ominous situation. As needed, help children write to publish a book of "Ominous Tales."

WOW! Rhyme: **ominous**

An ominous look is all it took.
An ominous call would silence
    them all.
That ominous sky meant none would
    be dry.
'Twas a warning that threatened
those campers that night.
'Twas a worrisome wait—
'Twas an ominous sight.

Here's What It Means

adjective: likeable looks and behavior

Synonyms—*They have nearly the same meaning.*

attractive   pleasing
lovely   presentable
pleasant

Forms of *personable* to Share with 7s

personably (adverb)

Talk & Share

1. The tour guide seemed quite personable.
2. I try to be personable to everyone during a disagreement.
3. The personable officer helped us cross the street.
4. Mom leaves personable notes in my lunch kit.
5. I don't act personably if I haven't had enough sleep.
6. The radio announcer had a personable voice.
7. Our mail carrier always smiles and is really personable.
8. If I behave personably, I know I'll win friends.
9. The personable storyteller acted out each character's part.
10. It's difficult to be personable when I'm really hungry.

Focusing Talk:
Identifying Personable Poses

Clip from magazines and newspapers various photos that show people in action. You may choose to use Web sites for pictures of people doing activities. Invite discussion about the photographed facial expressions and body language that give reason to think a person is personable or not. Remind children that each idea is merely a person's opinion. List ideas about personable-looking and not-so-personable-looking qualities.

Hands-On:
Publishing How-to-Be-Personable Books

Talk about the purposes of various "How-to" books found in bookstores and libraries. Help each child fold in half two blank sheets of paper to make a booklet. Invite children to reference and add to their list from the above activity as they write and/or illustrate a how-to book of ways to be personable and attract friends. Have children title their books "How to Make Friends," "How to Gain Friends," or "Ways to Have Friends."

WOW! Rhyme: **personable**

I like kind things I see him do.
He says, "Hello"
to me and you.
I like how helpful he can be.
He seems quite personable, to me.

Here's What It Means

noun: point of view

Synonyms—*They have nearly the same meaning.*

feelings   viewpoint

outlook   way of thinking

position

Figuratively Speaking

attitude

Talk & Share

1. My perspective is that it's too cold to play outside.

2. I'd like to get everyone's perspective before we make any decisions.

3. Dad's perspective is that it costs too much money!

4. My perspective is that I always shop for the best buy.

5. Grandma's perspective about music differs from mine.

6. From my perspective, it looks like you don't care.

7. Could you share your perspective so I can understand how you feel?

8. Let's ask the eyewitness to share her perspective.

9. Sy shared a different perspective than we'dexpected.

10. It's interesting to have a fresh perspective on the idea.

Focusing Talk:
Comparing Perspectives

Tell children how eyewitnesses tell their perspectives of a happening. Have three witnesses leave the room as the group plans a scenario, such as: Two children drop pencils and argue about ownership as a third child claims a pencil and a fourth child complains of being poked with a pencil. Invite the witnesses to return, watch the scenario closely, and then tell and compare their perspectives. Repeat for more complex scenarios.

Hands-On:
Writing from a Perspective

Remind children that for every idea or event, there are many people who have written to share their unique perspectives on the topic. Have children do Internet research to find three writers' perspectives on the life of a famous person, a historical event, or an idea. Have partners share and compare their authors' perspectives. At another time, have children gain perspectives on a dance or piece of music from folks of three age stages.

WOW! Rhyme: **perspective**

It's only my perspective.

This doesn't mean it's true.

It's only my perspective

which means it's my own view.

Here's What It Means

adjective: important to the topic

Synonyms—*They have nearly the same meaning.*

appropriate	necessary
connected	related
fitting	suitable

Figuratively Speaking

to the point

Forms of *pertinent* to Share with 7s

pertain (verb)
pertinence (noun)

Talk & Share

1. Correct diet is pertinent to the care of a pet snake.

2. It's pertinent that you tell me your shoe size if I'm buying you new shoes.

3. Mom said it was pertinent to tell the gym teacher that I hurt my ankle.

4. That detail has pertinence to the police officer's investigation.

5. Native Americans taught the pilgrims pertinent survival information.

6. The problems on our science test ask for pertinent facts about the planets.

7. It is pertinent to study adaptations to understand an animal.

8. Does that question even pertain to our discussion?

9. Information about early explorers is pertinent to a study of our history.

10. The poster lists pertinent information about class procedures.

Focusing Talk:
Identifying Pertinent Words

Write a familiar word inside an oval on the board. Begin a word web by writing the word's definition in a second oval that branches off. Help children note words within the definition that are pertinent when using the word in a sentence to add another branched oval. Help children look for words pertinent to a discussion of this webbed word. Other web branches may group pertinent words, such as synonyms, sounds like, or used with.

Hands-On:
Noting Pertinent Information

Help children apply *pertinent* and *pertinence* to make a KWL Chart with column headers, Know?, Want to Know?, and Learned. Introduce a topic and provide pertinent materials children can use to take a picture walk, list pertinent information they know or want to know, and then read in order to fill in the third column with pertinent new information. Throughout the activity, help children ask, "Does this information pertain to the topic?"

> ### WOW! Rhyme: **pertinent**
>
> Is it pertinent here?
> Is it fitting to use?
> Let's get to the point—
> we need pertinent news!

Here's What It Means

noun: what gets put ahead of other things

Synonyms—*They have nearly the same meaning.*

top idea in a list
something that comes first

Figuratively Speaking

get things straight; get it together

Forms of *priority* to Share with 7s

priorities (noun)
prioritize (verb)

Talk & Share

1. Improving my use of time is a priority this year.

2. My priorities are to finish my homework and go to sleep.

3. I need to make eating a priority before doing anything else.

4. Dad's homemade soup is a priority when we plan a dinner menu.

5. Fresh juice is a breakfast priority in our house.

6. Mom said to get my priorities in order, with chores at the top.

7. I plan to prioritize the things I need to do today.

8. I had to prioritize what I wanted to say to you about our disagreement.

9. Getting to bed on time is a high priority at my house.

10. Our priorities are the same as they were yesterday.

Focusing Talk: Identifying Priorities

Have children list their three most important chores at home. Then ask children to number those chores in order of their importance. Now, have children list and number three chore priorities their parents would likely name. Help children share and compare their own lists versus parent lists. Encourage discussion about reasons chore priorities may differ in different homes and may differ from the perspective of children versus parents.

Hands-On: Planning and Prioritizing

Provide five sheets of paper for each child. Ask children to use one paper to illustrate each of five activities they plan to do alone or with others in the coming week. Once completed, ask children to prioritize and number in order the drawings according to how they expect to do the activities. Then ask children to similarly prioritize and assign letters to the drawings in order of their importance or in order of personal enjoyment.

WOW! Rhyme: *priority*

Priorities!

Priorities!

My parents have priorities!

It's homework, piano, and tons of
   chores—

They all come first—*then* it's playing
   outdoors.

Priorities!

Priorities!

Why must they have priorities?

Here's What It Means

adjective: productive; plentiful

Synonyms—*They have nearly the same meaning.*

abundant
fruitful

Figuratively Speaking

lotsa

Talk & Share

1. Needra's a prolific reader, so she goes to the library often.

2. The prolific rain forests are home to countless numbers of plants and animals.

3. The prolific sellers posted signs that helped us find all the garage sales.

4. Mozart, a prolific composer of classical music, lived from 1756 to 1791.

5. Hank Aaron was a prolific hitter of home runs.

6. I like it when I have prolific choices during free time.

7. Knights and castles were prolific in Europe during the Middle Ages.

8. Grandpa's prolific tree produced more pears last year than we could eat.

9. The prolific frogs filled the creek by my house with their families.

10. Prolific painters worked in the years following the Middle Ages.

Focusing Talk: Identifying Prolific Ideas

Read aloud *The 500 Hats of Bartholomew Cubbins* (see Resources, page 173). Ask children how the word *prolific* might apply to the story (number of hats; challenges for Bartholomew; Bartholomew's patience and positive thinking; the fun language of Dr. Seuss; etc.). Help children name prolific ideas they've noticed around them. Point out that this Dr. Seuss book differs from his usual books in that it's written in prose, rather than in rhyme.

Hands-On: Noting Prolific Castles

Using Internet sites, such as http://www.castles.org/castles or http://www.hearstcastle.org, talk about the world's prolific castles. Then invite partners to select a country and print exterior views of each of five or more of that country's castles. Help partners label each castle by its name and country. Compile the pages alphabetically by country and then by castle name. Bind and title the collection.

> **WOW! Rhyme: prolific**
>
> I am a prolific talker.
> I always have lots to say.
> I'm also a prolific reader.
> I read a new book every day.

Here's What It Means

adjective: likely to happen

Another Meaning

adjective: lying flat, often facedown

Synonyms—*They have nearly the same meaning.*

apt   probably will
liable to   tend to

Talk & Share

1. Freddy is prone to having temper tantrums.

2. The baby preferred to sleep in the prone position.

3. We are prone to breezes along the shoreline.

4. Our principal is prone to forgive and excuse a student's first poor choice.

5. People were prone to doubt Columbus when he claimed the world was round.

6. In many European countries, children are prone to speak two languages.

7. My Grandpa is prone to talk about his years as a college football star.

8. Are you prone to remember names of people you meet?

9. I'm prone to play outside when the weather's nice.

10. Gif is prone to do his homework right after school.

Focusing Talk:
Identifying Prone Happenings

Present scenarios, such as the following, and help children tell what would be prone to happen: someone who doesn't tie shoelaces (prone to falls); person who studies for tests (prone to earn good grades); someone who bullies or gossips (prone to have few friends); someone who likes to read (prone to read often). Then engage children in brainstorming ways to change a negative situation into one that is prone to reap positive results.

Hands-On:
Dramatizing Prone Behaviors

Help children make finger puppets, using instructions, such as those available at: http://www.starwars.com/kids/do/crafts/f20090402.html or http://www.ehow.com/how_2098389_make-finger-puppets.html. Invite children to use finger puppets to dramatize scenarios in which one puppet helps another who is prone to being late, falling down, losing things, and so on. Children might work in teams or small groups and showcase performances in a community circle.

WOW! Rhyme: **prone**

**If you're prone to share
with those who lack,
you're prone to receive
lotsa kindness back.**

Here's What It Means

verb: to feel sorry about something

noun: a feeling of being sorry about something

Synonyms—*They have nearly the same meaning.*

to express an apology

disappointment

dissatisfaction

feel guilty

moan over

mourn

feel sorrow

Forms of *regret* to Share with 7s

regretful (adjective)

regrets (verb, noun)

regrettably (adverb)

regretted (verb)

regretting (verb)

Talk & Share

1. I regret acting angry with my friend, who was only trying to help me.

2. Samantha regretted cheating on the test.

3. Jora regretted telling me about the surprise party.

4. I enjoyed too much candy and am regretting it now.

5. It's getting so cold that Elizabeth regrets wearing shorts.

6. I'm regretful that I didn't ask the new kid to play.

7. Sisha regretted having to free his pet snake.

8. I decided to admit breaking the window so I would have no regrets.

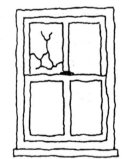

9. Regrettably, the bus broke down on the way to the field trip.

10. We regret that we are out of the ice cream flavor you chose.

Focusing Talk:
Talking about Regrets

Tell children about a time you felt regret for your actions or words. Help partners follow your model to take turns telling each other about times they felt sorry or regretful for actions or words. Provide a ruler or twig as a talking stick in a community circle. The one who holds the talking stick gets to talk as others listen. Encourage use of *regret* and its forms, and ask children to suggest a plan for how they might act in the future.

Hands-On:
Dramatizing a Series of Unfortunate Regrets

Ask children to help you prepare a stack of note cards, each telling an unfortunate event, such as *I broke a window; I lost my dad's racquet; I stepped on a friend's foot; I threw a ball that hit my mom's car; I excluded a friend from a game*; and so on. Have partners take turns acting or observing to guess the incident being dramatized and causing regretful feelings. Encourage use of forms of *regret*.

WOW! Rhyme: **regret**

My regrets?

I'll name a few:

I didn't say hello to you.

I watched TV too much last night.

I didn't try to stop our fight.

My regrets?

I've shared a few.

And now I ask,

"Hey! What about you?"

Here's What It Means

verb: to talk or write about things that happened in the past

Synonyms—*They have nearly the same meaning.*

look back   remember
recall   think back
recollect

Figuratively Speaking

hark back

Forms of *reminisce* to Share with 7s

reminisced (verb)
reminisces (verb)
reminiscing (verb)

Talk & Share

1. My teacher reminisced about times when she had homework in college.

2. We were reminiscing with old neighbors who came back to visit.

3. Sometimes my grandpa seems to reminisce too much.

4. My dads like to reminisce about when they traveled to adopt me.

5. Aunt Mayola thinks I'm too young to be reminiscing about my youth.

6. My parents are always reminiscing about when I was a baby.

7. When I go to college, maybe I'll reminisce about days at this school.

8. Uncle Julio reminisces about when he had hair.

9. It helps if we reminisce about how it felt to be a kindergartener.

10. I can't reminisce with you because I don't remember that time.

Focusing Talk:
Reminiscing Events of a Lifetime

Reminisce four events in your life to share with children phases in your life. Reminisce using ordering words, such as, "As I reminisce, first I went swinging at the park. Second, I played field hockey in fifth grade. Third, I studied in my room at college. And fourth, I taught you yesterday!" If need be, repeat the model, using a close relative's lifetime. Then ask children to follow your model to reminisce four phases of their lives.

Hands-On:
Reminiscing to Illustrate a Life

In advance, ask family members to reminisce with children about parties and celebrations, trips, or cute or interesting behaviors children did as babies or toddlers. Provide each child a cover page and one front or back page for each year of their lives. Invite children to illustrate their cover and then draw, in consecutive order, pictures that are reminiscent of stories they've heard or reviewed in photos with family members.

WOW! Rhyme: *reminisce*

My grandmas reminisce about
the things they used to do.
They tell the same old, lengthy tales—
I never know who's who.

Right now, they're reminiscing.
My uncles and aunts are, too.
Ya think someone might reminisce—
and tell a tale that's new?

replenish (ri PLEN ish)

Here's What It Means

verb: to make full again

Synonyms—*They have nearly the same meaning.*

refill   replace
refresh   restock
reload   restore
renew

Forms of *replenish* to Share with 7s

replenishable (adjective)
replenished (adjective, verb)
replenishes (verb)
replenishing (verb)

Talk & Share

1. We need to replenish our supply of paper napkins before the picnic.

2. Mom asked me to replenish her glass of lemonade.

3. A drink of water and a short rest replenished my energy.

4. Grandpa says the fertilizer is replenishing the nutrients in his garden.

5. Trees are a replenishable resource, while oil is not replenishable.

6. Recycling newspaper replenishes the paper supply without cutting down trees.

7. George Washington had difficulty replenishing his army's supplies.

8. We replenished our pile of firewood before the snow came.

9. Water is replenishable when the water cycle isn't interrupted.

10. Bring more pencils to replenish your supply tomorrow.

Focusing Talk: Discussing Replenishment

Read aloud *The Lorax* (see Resources, page 173). Encourage discussion about the Truffula Trees and whether they can be replenished. Talk about how Dr. Seuss's Truffula Tree is a metaphor that calls to our minds the silent request by Earth's natural resources to prevent their demise or, if need be, work to replenish them. Help children research natural resources, ways to replenish each, and ways to prevent the need for replenishment.

Studying Plans for Replenishment

Have each of four small groups select the recycling Web site at http://earth911.com/, choose a different item (plastic, paper, metal, glass), and discuss ways to recycle the item. Help each group display recycling ideas on a bulletin board. Share http://www.unep.org/billiontreecampaign/pledges/ and discuss how monies earned from recycling can help replant trees as part of the United Nations' Billion Tree Campaign.

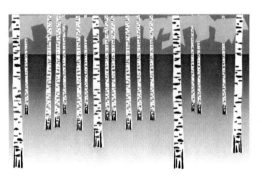

WOW! Rhyme: *replenish*

Replenish the paper?
Replenish the ink?
We need to replenish
this printer, I think!

Here's What It Means

adjective: happening at the same time

Synonyms—*They have nearly the same meaning.*

in unison
together

Form of *simultaneous* to Share with 7s

simultaneously (adverb)

Talk & Share

1. If we push simultaneously, we may be able to move the heavy box.

2. The wind made the two swings sway simultaneously.

3. Dad heard our simultaneous "Yes!" when he asked if we wanted ice cream.

4. Can you pat your head and rub your stomach simultaneously?

5. The streetlights come on simultaneously at six o'clock.

6. I can't do homework and watch television simultaneously.

7. With a simultaneous wave, we said our good-byes.

8. At midnight, we heard a howl that seemed simultaneous with the clock's chime.

9. My classmates greet one another simultaneously each morning.

10. I look for a rainbow when I see sunshine and rain simultaneously.

Focusing Talk:
Discussing Simultaneous Actions

Invite children to take note of behaviors they do simultaneously or as groups of two or more. Examples might include eating lunch, shaking hands, reciting poems or songs, breathing, or blinking. Invite children to try out their ideas. Talk about actions that, if done simultaneously, might cause problems or danger. Examples include two persons up at bat, typing two computer keys, two persons talking, or two planes in the same air space.

Singing Simultaneously

Sing "Down by the Bay" (see Resources, page 174). Invite children to participate simultaneously to sing the chorus. Repeat the song until children are comfortable in joining in simultaneously. Then model how one might make up a new and original rhyming verse to insert into the song. Invite partners to create and share simultaneously an original rhyming verse for the whole group to join in simultaneously on the chorus.

WOW! Rhyme: *simultaneous*

If I reach out
my hand to you,
and you reach out to me,
I'm greeting you.
You're greeting me.
Hey!
Simultaneously!

Here's What It Means

verb: to give support; to make it last a long time

Synonyms—*They have nearly the same meaning.*

carry on	hold up
continue	keep up
endure	maintain
feed	preserve

Forms of *sustain* to Share with 7s

sustainable (adjective)

sustained (verb)

sustaining (verb)

sustains (verb)

sustenance (noun)

Talk & Share

1. The singer sustained the high note for a long time.

2. Can she sustain that speed all the way to the finish line?

3. A good breakfast should sustain my energy throughout the morning.

4. The coach is effective in sustaining the players' enthusiasm.

5. We seek unpolluted air because our air is a sustainable natural resource.

6. Beaches can be sustained when sand dunes are built on old pine trees.

7. I'm hungry and looking for some sustenance.

8. Its wide base sustains the weight of that large statue.

9. Worms are decomposers that sustain good soil.

10. I am sustaining the plant with sunlight, water, and air.

Focusing Talk: Choosing Sustenance

Using an analog clock, demonstrate counting seconds and minutes by fives. Engage partners in making predictions about how long they can sustain an action, such as to hold up an arm, wave, be silent, or pace the floor. Help partners use forms of *sustain* to tell how long and why they chose to sustain actions. Discuss how people and animals in all parts of the world make choices of food, water, and shelter to sustain their lives.

Hands-On: Creating Sustainable Environments

To make a terrarium, cut across a clear two-liter bottle 6 inches above its base. In the base, layer 1 inch of small stones, 2 inches of rich soil, and small plants, moss, dried leaves, twigs, and so on. Add 1 tablespoon of water. Then cut eight vertical slits 2 inches down, fold slits over one another, and slide the capped top section onto the bottom. Set in sunlight. Observe how air and water cycle around. Add worms or pill bugs to decompose dead leaves and sustain the soil.

WOW! Rhyme: **sustain**

One sun sustains us all.

It grows the wheat we use for bread.

It grows the grass so cows get fed.

The cows may then become our meat.

All living things on Earth must eat.

One sun sustains it all.

tedious (TEE dee uhs)

Here's What It Means

adjective: long and boring

Synonyms—*They have nearly the same meaning.*

dreary   unexciting

dull   uninteresting

over and over again

Figuratively Speaking

BOR-ING!, detailed

Forms of *tedious* to Share with 7s

tediously (adverb)

tediousness (noun)

Talk & Share

1. Waiting in a long line can feel very tedious.

2. Raking leaves in our backyard is a tedious job.

3. I tediously wrote each spelling word five times.

4. My teacher's jokes make studying seem less tedious.

5. My mom loves to paint walls, but I think it's a tedious job.

6. To break up the tediousness of this rainy day, I baked cookies.

7. I find it tedious to watch a snake but fun to watch a hamster.

8. I think shelving library books would be a tedious job.

9. I sing to myself to take the tediousness out of pulling weeds.

10. He tediously stitched ten buttons onto the shirt.

Focusing Talk:
Identifying Tedious Activities

Invite children to discuss tedious experiences, such as eating the same food or performing the same chore every day. Help children discuss jobs they see adults doing and whether such jobs may or may not seem tedious when children consider future careers. Remind children that different folks like different things. Invite a thumbs-up if children would not find a particular career tedious and a thumbs-down if they would see that job boring.

Hands-On:
Erasing Unnecessary Tediousness

Have children list in their journals a tedious school-day experience, along with ways to erase such tediousness. Gather children into a community circle to share journal entries. Record all ideas, and post the list for children's personal use in erasing tedium while doing necessary tasks. Ask for ideas that could bring less tedium to a school day. Ideas might include singing "Today's Song" (see Resources, page 174) or solving a daily riddle.

WOW! Rhyme: **tedious**

'Tis a tedious task
that I must do.
It's tedious
and boring
and dull.

So what's new?

Here's What It Means

noun: actions and beliefs passed on to younger folks

Synonyms—*They have nearly the same meaning.*

custom	ritual
habit	routine
legend	something always done
practice	standard

Forms of *tradition* to Share with 7s

traditional (adjective)
traditionally (adverb)

Talk & Share

1. Some have a tradition of removing their shoes before going inside.
2. Mom's traditional remedy for a cold is to serve chicken soup.
3. The Bulldogs traditionally win, but the Ravens won the game this year.
4. Grandma has a tradition of scattering our cut hair on her garden.
5. Some families traditionally serve turkey on Thanksgiving.
6. If we teach children to recycle, maybe reusing things will become a tradition.
7. Breaking a piñata is a birthday tradition for Javier's family.
8. People came to America to gain freedom to practice their religious traditions.
9. Some people gather for traditional reunions.
10. Traditionally, our school's fifth graders have their picnic in May.

Focusing Talk: Discussing Traditions

On butcher paper, use quilt-like dashes to draw a 9-inch-by-9-inch space for each child. Invite children to share traditions their families enjoy during holidays or special events, such as a birthday, Superbowl Sunday, or even the loss of a tooth. Help children pencil in the center of their grids, their names, an event, and a bulleted list of traditions for that event. Discuss how events and celebrations differ from family to family. Use this record for the next activity.

Hands-On: Creating a Traditions Quilt

Provide each child an 8-inch-by-8-inch sheet of manila paper. Have children write headings, such as "The Smiths' Thanksgiving," to identify their family name and the event from above activity. Children might illustrate headings. To complete a "Traditions Quilt," attach children's drawings to their grid spaces from the above activity such that bulleted notes are covered. The above activity's dashed grid lines will then appear similar to a quilt's stitching.

WOW! Rhyme: **tradition**

We've always done it
just this way
from years ago until today;
and doing so gives us permission
to title it
as our tradition.

Here's What It Means

adjective: peaceful

Synonyms—*They have nearly the same meaning.*

calm	still
calmness	stillness
quiet	undisturbed

Figuratively Speaking

sea of tranquility

Form of *tranquil* to Share with 7s

tranquility (noun)

Talk & Share

1. It's tranquil at my house when our baby is asleep.

2. Dad thinks tranquility is the best part of being in a canoe.

3. I like to have a tranquil place to do my homework.

4. It's easier to think when things are tranquil.

5. I like the tranquility I sense just before falling asleep.

6. Astronauts explored a place on the moon called the Sea of Tranquility.

7. I gave my mom some tranquility on Mother's Day.

8. My room feels tranquil when my bed is made.

9. Dinner time is generally tranquil at my house.

10. It's impossible to feel tranquil when I'm tired and hungry.

Focusing Talk:
Exploring a Sea of Tranquility

Read aloud the following Internet site, adding drama and defining words as needed: http://www.nasa.gov/directorates/esmd/home/19jul_seaoftranquillity.html. Help children use forms of *tranquil* and synonyms to tell about times they have experienced a "sea of tranquility" here on Earth. Encourage a variety of locations and times of day. Ask what factors helped to make each experience seem tranquil.

Hands-On:
Picturing Tranquility

Have children explore magazines and newspapers in search of illustrations and photos that depict tranquility. Invite children to illustrate ideas of tranquil times and tranquil places. Have children autograph their illustrations and add captions. At another time, help children explore the following Web sites to view the word *tranquility* in Japanese and in Chinese: http://japanese.about.com/bl50kanji6_heion.htm and http://www.chinese-symbols.com/t-chinese-symbol-for-tranquility.

WOW! Rhyme: *tranquil*

I like it when it's tranquil—
when there's calmness all around me.
When there's stillness,
I feel peaceful.
I enjoy tranquility.

transparent (trans PAIR uhnt)

Here's What It Means
adjective: easy to see through

Synonyms—*They have nearly the same meaning.*

clear	lets light pass through
easily understood	not solid
fine or delicate in texture	obvious

Figuratively Speaking
full of hot air; transparent

Form of *transparent* to Share with 7s
transparency (noun)

Talk & Share

1. Mom's delicate black scarf is transparent.

2. Her offer to be my friend seemed transparent.

3. A single sheet of tissue paper can be too transparent to wrap a gift.

4. My aunt likes the transparency of clear glass baking dishes.

5. Dad sets his favorite plants in front of our most transparent windows.

6. Newspaper comics are good for wrapping gifts because the pages are not transparent.

7. The water's transparency allowed us to see a colossal number of fish.

8. My mom wears a slip under one skirt because the skirt is too transparent.

9. Some find that transparent solar windows save energy.

10. I should have recognized the transparency in his offer to share.

Focusing Talk:
Noting Transparencies
Point to a transparent container and model saying, "This [item] is transparent. I know it's transparent because I can see through it to see the [item's content] inside." Have partners explore the room and hallways to similarly identify transparencies. Ask partners to record their items for use in reporting discoveries to the class. Encourage the activity with family members at home. Discuss offers of help or compliments that seem transparent or not sincerely intended as being kind or helpful.

Hands-On:
Testing for Transparency
Provide several scraps of assorted fabrics and papers for partners to sort from most transparent to least transparent. Remind children that holding items in front of a light source, such as a window or lamp, can be helpful in this activity. Invite children to use forms of *transparent* to identify each material and report how it "tested." Partners might compare their items and results and then regroup their combined items for transparency.

WOW! Rhyme: **transparent**

His reasons seem transparent,
so his tale may not be true.
But he's known for being truthful.
So, perhaps, he has no clue.

Here's What It Means

adjective: very dangerous

Synonyms—*They have nearly the same meaning.*

not trustworthy
surprisingly tricky
unreliable

Figuratively Speaking

a slippery slope; like being out on a limb;
like skating on thin ice

Forms of *treacherous* to Share with 7s

treacherously (adverb)
treacherousness (noun)
treachery (noun)

Talk & Share

1. We hiked a treacherous trail.

2. Pirates used to practice their treachery on the high seas.

3. Driving on mountain roads feels really treacherous to me.

4. The magician moved treacherously close to the flames.

5. The treacherousness of polluted waterways challenge salmon migration.

6. The trickster in this story is full of treachery.

7. Boating is a challenge in treacherous currents.

8. My baby sister's attempts to walk sometimes seem treacherous.

9. Mud can feel as treacherous as quicksand.

10. The treacherousness of the Gulf of Aden once earned it the name Pirate Alley.

Focusing Talk:
Identifying Treacherous Tricksters

Read aloud "Tricksters in Tales" (see Resources, page 182). Help children use forms of *treacherous* to identify each story's trickster and to talk about why each trickster apparently chose such treachery. Invite children to name other traitorous, treacherous characters in tales they've read or heard about. To help children retain familiarity with the referenced tales, you might include the tales as read-alouds throughout the year.

Hands-On:
Identifying Treacherous Waters

Read *The Gulls of the Edmund Fitzgerald* and sing "The Wreck of the *Edmund Fitzgerald*" (see Resources, pages 173– 174). Provide a U.S. map for children to locate Lake Superior and other treacherous waters, such as the Colorado, Ohio, Mississippi, and Missouri rivers, California's Kern River, and the Northwest's Columbia River. Help list living and non-living factors that cause such treacherousness (alligators, plants, rocks, sandbars, falls).

WOW! Rhyme: **treacherous**

'Tis a treacherous tale
of a treacherous lake
'Tis a tale not forgotten
in many a town.
'Tis a treacherous tale
of a treacherous storm
on a treacherous night
when the *Edmund* went down.

Here's What It Means

verb: to prove

Synonyms—*They have nearly the same meaning.*

confirm   present evidence
make sure   show proof

Figuratively Speaking

make good; swear it's true; vouch for; check it out

Forms of *verify* to Share with 7s

verifiable (adjective)
verification (noun)
verified (verb, adjective)
verifies (verb)
verifying (verb)

Talk & Share

1. The number of passengers is verifiable by the number of tickets sold.

2. Dad verified that he is the owner of our car.

3. The clerk asked Mom for verification before she could use her debit card.

4. My lack of energy verifies that I didn't sleep well last night.

5. I am here to verify whatever my sister tells you.

6. Let's verify the rules by reading the game's instructions.

7. Grannie showed the technician a paper as verification of her warranty.

8. I can easily verify whether or not you can swim.

9. We'll be verifying how many egg cartons we need yet.

10. My identity is verified when I show my passport.

Focusing Talk:
Discussing Identity Verification

Talk about times when a name or other identification had to be verified to do an activity. Examples may include: getting into a pool or gym area, a concert, or other public place; using a credit or debit card; entering a country's border; withdrawing money from a bank account; and so on. Talk about why each verification is important. Talk about the importance of verification and privacy of personal information when using the Internet.

Hands-On:
Creating Identity Verification

Provide 2-inch-by-4-inch cardstock for each child to create a "business card" for a book or story character. You might present some business cards for models as children discuss and verify the kinds of information they might want to write on each character's card. Children may choose to add a drawing or logo-sized replica of the book's cover. This activity, like a book report, may be used as a child's verification of having read a book.

WOW! Rhyme: **verify**

It's easy to verify
that I'm really me.
I look in a mirror—
It's me that I see.
It's verification.
It's verified... see?
I am who I am.
I really am me!

Here's What It Means

noun: strength or energy

Synonyms—*They have nearly the same meaning.*

eagerness   power
enthusiasm   robustness
pep   spirit

Figuratively Speaking

get up and go; moxie; oomph; pluck; spunk;
staying power

Forms of *vigor* to Share with 7s

vigorous (adjective)
vigorously (adverb)

Talk & Share

1. Grampie says I am full of vim and vigor.

2. I agreed with my friend and vigorously
   supported his idea.

3. Our dance team is full of vigor.

4. Some mornings I don't feel as vigorous as
   on other days.

5. My family works vigorously to preserve
   our planet's resources.

6. I want to finish the race,
   so I'll run with vigor.

7. I often debate with
   vigor my reasons for
   staying up later.

8. Our coach wants us
   to be more vigorous
   about being on time
   for practice.

9. I have been practicing vigorously for my
   piano recital.

10. My baby brother has a vigorous grip on
    my finger.

Focusing Talk:
Describing Vigorous Feelings

Tell children of a time when you
felt vigorous about an idea as compared to an
idea that left you with no feelings of vigor. An
example might be a picnic plan on a day when
your refrigerator was full of food versus a day
when you had no picnic supplies in the house.
Help children use forms of *vigor* to similarly
compare and contrast times and reasons they did
or did not have vigorous feelings for an idea. Ideas
need not be related.

Hands-On:
Depicting Vigorous Activities

Invite children to draw or cut and paste
pictures or materials, such as beans, seeds, or
twigs, to depict a family member doing a favorite
activity with vigor. Talk about how some folks
appear more vigorous than others when doing
the same activity. For example, a baby or senior
may show a determined or flushed face when
trying to stand or sit, as compared to an older
child's face. Ask children to share their exhibits
with another class.

WOW! Rhyme: **vigor**

I was vigorously trying
to strike at the ball.
I tried.
And I tried.
I gave it my all.

Did I use too much vigor?
Did you see that ball?
I felt my bat cr-r-ack—
then I felt myself fall...

BLACKLINE MASTERS

WOW! Word Patterns

WOW! Word patterns provide a record-keeping option for users of *WOW! Words*. Although *WOW! Words* is a totally oral program, many users like the option to display the words in some fashion that shows at-a-glance the *WOW! Words* children have "met" orally. This makes it more likely that you will continue over time to toss familiar *WOW! Words* into conversations with children.

Record keeping is optional. Personally, I've had years when I've used *WOW! Words* all year long without using any accompanying visual presentation. More often, I've found the visual aid of a *WOW! Words* display useful in my record keeping and as an at-a-glance reminder to use *WOW! Words* in daily conversations with children.

The intent behind the blackline masters is to provide you with four different *WOW! Word* visuals, so that you can use this book for four years in a row with the same child or children (as in home use, a multi-age classroom, homeschooling use, or in a special needs classroom) and have a different display to present for children each year. Another reason for the four different and distinct

patterns is to provide you with choices over your own years of use. In my experience, children often like to choose a design to use for the entire year.

The following are segmented patterns for your choice of a different display for each of four age levels. You can display each on a wall and add one new "segment" each week. You may choose to write the new week's *WOW! Word* on the segment. As weeks pass, the *WOW! Word* display grows in length as it wends its way, segment by segment, across the wall or around the room. I've often displayed the *WOW! Word* "record" just above the classroom's chalk, bulletin, or white board. At home, a *WOW! Word* display might decorate the kitchen or family room, spaces that tend to invite verbal interactions among family members.

Each pattern fits onto paper that is 8½ inches by 11 inches. This size allows you to copy the page onto cardstock or colored paper and cut out the patterned segment. Please note that rotating some cut-out segments 90 degrees allows you to slip a new segment behind the previous one. This arrangement can provide space to write the week's *WOW! Word* across or up and down the segment.

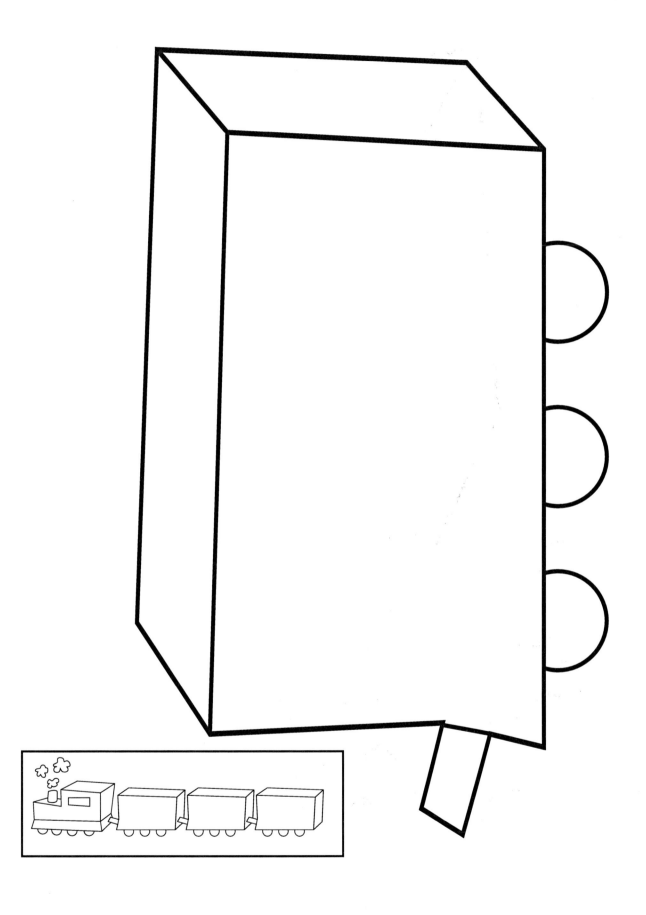

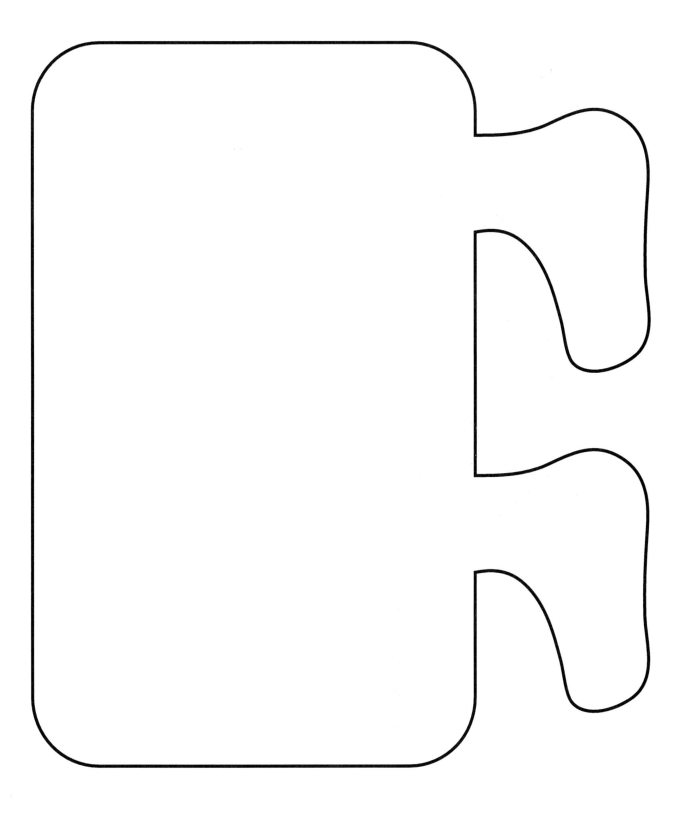

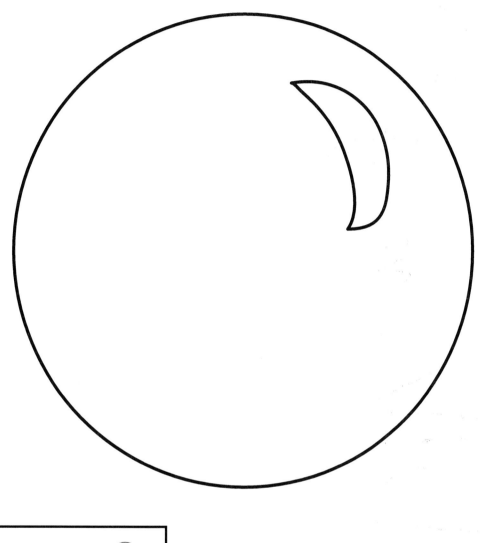

Letter to Family Members

Date _____

WOW! Word™ (*W*ord *O*f the *W*eek): _____

Some of its forms:

Dear Family Members,

Your child is learning how to use a special big word this week. Your child's ease in using this word is likely to cause you or another listener to say, "Wow!" Like each of us, your child likes this kind of positive, respectful attention. Your child gains confidence and looks for ways to learn more words to use in more conversations.

We know that good listeners and speakers become good readers and writers. So our goal in sharing *WOW! Words*—a *W*ord *O*f the *W*eek and one or more of its forms—is to help your child become that confident listener and speaker... with no expectation to read, write, or spell these big words. (If a child notices his or her own ability to read, write, or spell a WOW! Word, we simply say, "Wow!" and move on. This helps us focus on your child's many listening and speaking successes.) With each new WOW! Word, your child is learning a fun and meaningful WOW! Rhyme™ that the two of you can say together at home.

Your child may want to write, draw, or cut and glue a picture on this note to share thoughts about the use of this week's WOW! Word. Collecting the WOW! Words notes and pictures in a folder throughout the year will help the two of you remember to keep having fun and meaningful conversations with all 36 WOW! Words and their WOW! Rhymes this year.

Sincerely,

WOW! Words and *WOW! Rhyme* are trademarks of Babs Bell Hajdusiewicz.

RESOURCES

Books and Collections

Picture Books, Early Readers, and Chapter Books

The 500 Hats of Bartholomew Cubbins by Dr. Seuss. Random House, 1989. (*prolific*, 7s)

Amelia Bedelia series by Peggy Parish and Herman Parish. HarperCollins, 2003. (*literally*, 6s)

The Bridge Is Up! by Babs Bell Hajdusiewicz. HarperCollins, 2004. (*vehicle*, 4s)

Cars and Trucks and Things That Go by Richard Scarry. Golden Books, 1974. (*vehicle*, 4s)

The Cat in the Hat by Dr. Seuss. Random House, 1957. (*reluctant*, 6s)

The Cat in the Hat Comes Back by Dr. Seuss. Houghton Mifflin, 1958. (*perturbed*, 6s)

Chicka, Chicka, Boom Boom by Bill Martin, Jr. Little Simon, 2006. (*anticipate*, 5s)

Corduroy by Don Freeman. Viking 1968; Puffin, 1976. (*original*, 5s)

Curious George books by Hans Augusto Rey. Houghton Mifflin, 1973. (*curious*, 4s)

David's Father by Robert N. Munsch. Annick Press, 1983. (*anticipate*, 5s)

Each Peach Pear Plum by Allen Ahlberg. Viking, 1986. (*anticipate*, 5s)

The Frog Prince by Brothers Grimm, adapted by Sindy McKay. We Both Read Books by Treasure Bay, 1997. (*alternative*, 7s)

The Gulls of the Edmund Fitzgerald by Tres Seymour. Orchard, 1996. (*treacherous*, 7s)

Harold and the Purple Crayon by Crockett Johnson. Purple Crayon Books, 1989. (*resemble*, 5s)

In a Dark, Dark Room and Other Scary Stories by Alvin Schwartz. Harper Collins, 1985. (*ominous*, 7s)

It Looked Like Spilt Milk by Charles G. Shaw. (*resemble*, 5s)

Little Cloud by Eric Carle. Picture Puffins, 2001. (*resemble*, 5s)

The Lorax by Dr. Seuss. Random House Books for Young Readers, 1971. (*replenish*, 7s)

Make Way for Ducklings by Robert McCloskey. Penguin, 1999. (*threaten*, 5s)

A Mighty Knight by Babs Bell Hajdusiewicz. Rigby/ Houghton Mifflin Fold-Out Book, 1997.

My Faces by Babs Bell Hajdusiewicz. Dominie Press/ PearsonLearning, 1997. See also poem text on page 79. (*frantic*, 5s)

The Mysterious Giant of Barletta: An Italian Folktale by Tomie dePaola. Houghton Mifflin, 1984. (*colossal*, 7s)

Pierre: A Cautionary Tale in Five Chapters and a Prologue by Maurice Sendak. HarperCollins, 1991. (*nonchalant*, 7s)

Quick as a Cricket by Audrey Wood and Don Wood. Child's Play International, 1982. (*resemble*, 5s)

Rapunzel by Catherine McCafferty. Brighter Child, 2001. (*accessible*, 7s)

Rapunzel by Paul O. Zelinsky and Brothers Grimm. Puffin, 2002. (*accessible*, 7s)

The Recess Queen by Alexis O'Neill, Scholastic, 2002. (*intimidate*, 7s)

Scary Stories to Read When It's Dark by Arnold Lobel. SeaStar Books, 2000. (*ominous*, 7s)

Sputter, Sputter, Sput! by Babs Bell (Hajdusiewicz). HarperCollins, 2008. (*consume*, 5s; *vehicle*, 4s) See also the poem text on page 181.

Squirmy Earthworm by Babs Bell Hajdusiewicz. Rigby/Houghton Mifflin Fold-Out Book, 1997.

Stephanie's Ponytail by Robert N. Munsch. Annikins, 2007. (*anticipate*, 5s)

Stone Soup by Marcia Brown. Aladdin, 1986. (*contribute*, 4s)

The Story of Ferdinand by Munro Leaf. Viking, 1936. (*nonchalant*, 7s)

There's a Nightmare in My Closet by Mercer Mayer. Puffin, 1992. (*threaten*, 5s)

Tikki Tikki Tembo by Arlene Mosel. Square Fish, 2007. (*accessible*, 7s)

When Mindy Saved Hanukkah by Eric Kimmel. Scholastic, 1998. (*reluctant*, 6s)

You Have a Friend, Dainty Dinosaur by Babs Bell Hajdusiewicz. Modern Curriculum Press/ PearsonLearning, 1988. (*perturbrd*, 6s)

Poetry and Song Collections

Down by the Bay: A Traditional Song. Good Year Books, 1994. (*simultaneous*, 7s)

Down by the Bay—Raffi Songs to Read. Crown Books for Young Readers, 1988. (*simultaneous*, 7s)

Hajdusiewicz, Babs Bell. *Don't Go Out in Your Underwear!* Dominie Press/PearsonLearning, 1997. (*realistic*, 5s)

Hajdusiewicz, Babs Bell. *More! Phonics Through Poetry: Teaching Phonemic Awareness Using Poetry.* Good Year Books, 1999.

Hajdusiewicz, Babs Bell. *Phonics Through Poetry: Teaching Phonemic Awareness Using Poetry.* Good Year Books, 1999.

Hopkins, Lee Bennett. *Side by Side: Poems to Read Together.* Simon and Schuster, 1988. (*realistic*, 5s)

Prelutsky, Jack. *The Random House Book of Poetry for Children.* Random House, 1983. (*realistic*, 5s)

Prelutsky, Jack. *Read-aloud Rhymes for the Very Young.* Knopf, 1986. (*realistic*, 5s)

Silverstein, Shel. *A Light in the Attic.* Harper & Row, 1981. (*realistic*, 5s)

Silverstein, Shel. *Where the Sidewalk Ends.* Harper & Row, 1974. (*exaggerate*, 4s; *realistic*, 5s)

Traditional Stories, Fairy Tales, and Folktales

"The Frog Prince" by Brothers Grimm. See also Picture Books, Early Readers, and Chapter Books. (*alternative*, 7s)

"The Little Red Hen" (*diligent*, 7s)

"Little Red Riding Hood" (*threaten*, 5s)

"Mary Poppins" stories by P. L. Travers. Harcourt Odyssey, 1981. (*ridiculous*, 4s)

"Rapunzel" by Brothers Grimm, see also Picture Books. (*accessible*, 7s)

"The Reluctant Dragon" by Kenneth Grahame. From *Dream Days* by Kenneth Grahame. 1898. (*reluctant*, 6s)

"Rumpelstiltskin" (*summarize*, 5s)

"The Shepherd Boy and the Wolf" ("The Boy Who Cried Wolf") by Aesop. Ashton, R., compiler, and B. Higton, ed. *Aesop's Fables: A Classic Illustrated Edition.* Chronicle, 1990. (*urgent*, 4s; *alert*, 5s)

Stone Soup by Marcia Brown. Aladdin, 1986. (*contribute*, 4s)

"The Three Bears" (*summarize*, 5s)

The Three Little Pigs/Los Tres Cerditos by Merce Escardo i Bas. Chronicle Books, 2006. (*threaten*, 5s)

"The Three Little Pigs," in *Classic Fairy Tales* retold by Michael Foreman. Sterling, 2005.

"The Tortoise and the Hare" (*diligent*, 7s)

Poems and Songs by Various Writers

"Boa Constrictor" from *Where the Sidewalk Ends* by Shel Silverstein. Harper & Row, 1974. (*exaggerate*, 4s)

"Farmer in the Dell" (*contribute*, 4s)

"Food Chain" from *Science Verse* by Jon Scieszka. Penguin, 2004. (*consume*, 5s)

"Friendly Frederick Fuddlestone" from *Whiskers & Rhymes* by Arnold Lobel. HarperCollins, 1988. (*aghast*, 7s)

"Goops" from *Goops and How to Be Them* by Gelett Burgess. Frederick A. Stokes, 1900. (*disgusting*, 4s)

"Hungry Mungry" from *Where the Sidewalk Ends* by Shel Silverstein. Harper & Row, 1974. (*exaggerate*, 4s)

"Today's Song" by Babs Bell Hajdusiewicz. From http://ilikeme.com/index.php?option=com_content&view=article&id=60&Itemid=55. (*tedious*, 7s)

"True Story," from *Where the Sidewalk Ends* by Shel Silverstein. Harper & Row, 1974. (*aghast*, 7s; *exaggerate*, 4s)

"The Wreck of the *Edmund Fitzgerald*" poem and song by Gordon Lightfoot. Moose Music, 1976. (*treacherous*, 7s)

Poem and Song Texts by Babs Bell Hajdusiewicz and Others

Afraidy Day (*empathize*, 7s)

Yesterday was "afraidy" day—
Afraid my best friend wouldn't play.
Afraid it'd thunder, rain, and hail.
Afraid I'd spill the garbage pail.
Afraid my teeth would get decayed.
Afraid I'd have to get first-aid.
Afraid my shirt was not okay.
Afraid my dog would run away.
Afraid my dad would get delayed.
Afraid… that I would be afraid!

Gee, I'm glad today's today!
I'm starting new!
      Hip!
        Hip!
          Hooray!

Copyright © 1997 Babs Bell Hajdusiewicz.
First published in *Phonics Through Poetry: Teaching Phonemic Awareness Using Poetry* by Babs Bell Hajdusiewicz. Good Year Books, 1999.

Alas! (*positive*, 4s; *advantage*, 6s; *hazardous*, 6s)

Jack and Jill
Went up the hill
To fetch a pail of water.
Jack fell down
And broke his crown,
But, alas!
Jill was wearing her seat belt!

Copyright © 1986 Babs Bell Hajdusiewicz.
First published in *Poetry Works!*, Modern
Curriculum Press/PearsonLearning, 1991.

Bend and Stretch (*flexible*, 5s)

Look at how my muscles bend
to make my body small.
Look at how my muscles bend
to make my body tall.

I bend.
I'm small.
I stretch.
I'm tall.
I bend and stretch.
And that's not all!

Look at how, without a sound,
my body can go round and round
without a sound,
around and round
without a sound.

Now look at how my body can
without a sound
go round and round,
and round and round.
And watch my body;
watch it sit
without a sound,
without a sound.

Copyright © 2010 Babs Bell Hajdusiewicz.

Biography (*divulge*, 7s)

Biography is the category
For a person's real-life story.
Someone writes a story about
Another's life from inside out.

Copyright © 1992 Babs Bell Hajdusiewicz.
First published by Highsmith Upstart, Inc., 2005.

Bird Alert (*alert*, 5s)

Squirmy worms squirm
at the thought of getting hurt,
Or being served to baby birds
for dinner or dessert.

So squirmy worms take turns
serving duty in the dirt.
A squirmy worm on bird patrol
must blurt out, "Bird Alert!"

Copyright © 1999 Babs Bell Hajdusiewicz.
First published in *More! Phonics Through Poetry: Teaching
Phonemic Awareness Using Poetry* by Babs Bell Hajdusiewicz.
GoodYear Books, 1999.

The Bridge Is Up! (*vehicle*, 4s)

The bridge is up!
The bus can't go,
so everyone has to wait.
The bridge is up!
The bus can't go,
and the car can't go,
so everyone has to wait.
The bridge is up!
The bus can't go,
the car can't go,
and the bike can't go,
so everyone has to wait.
The bridge is up!
The bus can't go,
the car can't go,
the bike can't go,
and the truck can't go,
so everyone has to wait.
The bridge is up!
The bus can't go,
the car can't go,
the bike can't go,
the truck can't go,
and the motorcycle can't go,
so everyone has to wait.
The bridge is up!
The bus can't go,
the car can't go,
the bike can't go,
the truck can't go,
the motorcycle can't go,
and the bulldozer can't go,
so everyone has to wait.

The bridge is up!
The bus can't go,
the car can't go,
the bike can't go,
the truck can't go,
the motorcycle can't go,
the bulldozer can't go,
and the tractor can't go,
so everyone has to wait.
Now the bridge is down!
So the bus can go,
the car can go,
the bike can go,
the truck can go,
the motorcycle can go,
the bulldozer can go,
and the tractor can go!
Now nobody has to wait!

Bulldog Bully (*threaten*, 5s; *intimidate*, 7s)

Bulldog Billy was the neighborhood's bully.
He bullied everything in sight.
He bullied all the pullets till they ran to roost—
Then he bullied baby frogs all night.

Billy tried to bully two bulls in a field,
But Billy got ambushed, instead.
Two bullheaded bulls pushed Billy in the bushes—
Now Billy's off nursing his head!

Bunny Rabbit's Predicament (*predicament*, 4s)

Come along and meet Bunny!
He's a wee little rabbit
Who once upon a time, had a strange kind of habit.
He adored chewing gum from morning till night
And he often blew bubbles to his own delight.

But one day he blew a gum bubble so big
It popped, leaving Bunny with a thingamujig
Stuck to his whiskers, his nose, and his chin-
'Twas an awkward predicament Bunny was in!

Well, he squirmed
And he wiggled
And he snorted
And he sniffed
And he blew his gummy nose in his handkerchief.

And wouldn't you know, that hankie held tight.
It dangled from his nose like a parasite
Which caused Bunny's nose to begin to itch
And the itching caused the whiskers on Bunny to
    twitch.

Well, he squirmed
And he wiggled
And he snorted
And he sniffed
But his nose was still fastened to the handkerchief.

Well, along came a chum with a cupful of ice
Which he offered to the rabbit with some gummy
    advice:
"Your predicament is sticky but the gum will come
    off.
All we need is more ice from the watering trough."

"My, my, that's peculiar," said Bunny with a sigh,
"But my friend's here to help, so it can't hurt to try."
Then off hopped the rabbit and his chum to the
    trough,
Got the ice, froze the gum, and the hankie dropped
    off.

Now, the moral of the tale is "Never despair."
An unsolvable problem is generally rare.
Though you may need some help to get a job done,
'Cause two heads are sometimes better than one!

Circles (*numerous*, 4s)

Circles can roll round and round,
Round and round,
Round and round.
Circles can roll round and round
But squares and triangles can't!

Did You Ever See a Lassie? (*original*, 5s)

Did you ever see a lassie,
A lassie, a lassie?
Did you ever see a lassie
Go this way and that?
Go this way and that way,
And that way and this way,
Did you ever see a lassie
Go this way and that?

Did you ever see a laddie,
A laddie, a laddie?
Did you ever see a laddie
Go this way and that?
Go this way and that way,
And that way and this way,
Did you ever see a laddie
Go this way and that?

Traditional Nursery Song

Disorder (*disgusting*, 4s)

It's displeasing.
It's distasteful.
It's disruptive.
It's disgraceful.

This disorder,
though I've grown it,
is disgusting!
I disown it!

Copyright © 1998 Babs Bell Hajdusiewicz.
First published in *More! Phonics Through Poetry: Teaching Phonemic Awareness Using Poetry* by Babs Bell Hajdusiewicz. Good Year Books, 1999.

Earth Says (*thrifty*, 6s)

I'm giving you oodles of cues
To reduce, recycle, reuse.
It's time to refuse
The choice to abuse
Or lose your freedom to choose.

Copyright © 1989 Babs Bell Hajdusiewicz.
First published in *Poetry Works! The Second Stanza* by Babs Bell Hajdusiewicz. Modern Curriculum Press/ PearsonLearning, 1991.

Fiction (*realistic*, 5s; *divulge*, 7s)

In fiction, your imagination
Hasn't any limitation.
Dogs can talk and kids can fly
And no one has to justify.

Copyright © 1991 Babs Bell Hajdusiewicz.
First published in World Book WonderStorms, 1992.

Fighting Makes No Sense! (*tremendous*, 5s)

My ears and eyes
And nose and tongue
And fingers had a fight.
Each part of me said it was best
And each thought it was right.

"Sounds to hear are everywhere!"
My ears bragged to the rest.
"None of you can hear those sounds,
So that makes Ears the best!"

"Sights to see are everywhere!"
My eyes bragged to the rest.
"None of you can see those sights,
So that makes Eyes the best!"

"Smells to sniff are everywhere!"
My nose bragged to the rest.
"None of you can sniff those smells,
So that makes Nose the best!"

"Tastes to taste are everywhere!"
My tongue bragged to the rest.
"None of you can taste those tastes,
So that makes Tongue the best!"

"Things to touch are everywhere!"
My hands bragged to the rest.
"Our fingers touch and feel those things,
So that makes Fingers best!"

Then I said, "Fighting makes no sense!
All five of you are best!
Not one can do the other's job,
But… each sense helps the rest."

Copyright © 1992 Babs Bell Hajdusiewicz.
First published in *Poetry Works! The First Verse*, Modern Curriculum Press/PearsonLearning, 1992.

Humpty Dumpty (*positive*, 4s)

Humpty Dumpty sat on a wall.
Humpty Dumpty had a great fall.
All the King's horses,
And all the King's men
Couldn't put Humpty together again!

Traditional Nursery Rhyme

It's a Fact! (*disgusting*, 4s)

It's easy to spot them.
   Their manners are rude.
They talk while they're chewing.
   whole mouthfuls of food.

It's easy to spot them.
   They don't like to share.
They interrupt others.
   They brag and they swear.

It's easy to spot them.
   They never say, "Thanks."
They never say, "Sorry!"
   for meanness or pranks.

It's easy to spot them.
   They cut in a line.
They grab things from others
   with "Gimme! That's mine!"

It's easy to spot them—
   the way the Rudes act
is gross and disgusting
   and rude—it's a fact!

Copyright © 1997 by Babs Bell Hajdusiewicz.
First published in *Don't Go Out in Your Underwear!*
by Babs Bell Hajdusiewicz. Dominie Press/
PearsonLearning, 1997.

It's Not My Fault! (*perturbed*, 6s)

I try my best to be polite.
I know what's wrong and what is right.
But sometimes little parts of me
"act up" and "bug" my family.

My tongue sticks out.
My knuckles crunch.
My lips make smacking sounds at lunch.
My fingers poke and pinch and pick.
My feet jump out and trip or kick.
My mouth says words that aren't nice—
Today it spit… and tattled—twice!

It's not my fault that parts of me
act rude and "bug" my family!
So don't blame me for what they did!
It's not my fault! I'm just a kid!

Copyright © 1997 Babs Bell Hajdusiewicz.
First published in *Don't Go Out in Your Underwear!*
by Babs Bell Hajdusiewicz. Dominie Press/
PearsonLearning, 1997.

Jack Be Nimble (*hazardous*, 6s)

Jack be nimble,
Jack be quick,
Jack jump over the candlestick.

Traditional Nursery Rhyme

Let's Talk (*alternative*, 7s)

Let's not kick
   or hit or fight.
Let's find a way
   to make this right.
When you and I
   do not agree,
I'll talk to you.
   You talk to me.

Copyright © 1996 Babs Bell Hajdusiewicz.
First published in *Peaceful Me* by Babs Bell Hajdusiewicz.
Reading Realm, 2002.

Me a Mess? (*undoubtedly*, 5s)

Unclean and unbuckled,
Unfastened, untied,
Unfit to be seen,
I'm undignified.
Unfolded, unbuttoned,
Unbecoming, no less.
Unfortunately I'm
Unaware I'm a mess.

Copyright © 1989 Babs Bell Hajdusiewicz.
First published in *Poetry Works!* by Babs Bell Hajdusiewicz.
Modern Curriculum Press/PearsonLearning, 1990.

A Mighty Knight (*intention*, 6s)

In the daytime,
   a mighty knight
   fights mighty fights in the sunlight.
At nighttime,
   the mighty knight
   fights mighty fights by flashlight.
But at midnight,
   a mighty frightened knight
   goes nighty-night with a nightlight.

Copyright © 1997 Babs Bell Hajdusiewicz.
First published in *Don't Go Out in Your Underwear!*
by Babs Bell Hajdusiewicz. Dominie Press/PearsonLearning, 1997.
See also *A Mighty Knight* above under Picture Books,
Early Readers, and Chapter Books.

My Bones (*flexible*, 5s)

My skeleton tries its best to hide
But I can feel my bones inside
My arms
My legs
My shoulders
My toes
My ankles
My fingers
My knees
My nose
My skeleton tries its best to hide
But I can feel my bones inside!

Copyright © 1991, 2009 Babs Bell Hajdusiewicz.
First published in *Poetry Works! The First Verse,*
Modern Curriculum Press/PearsonLearning, 1992.

My Bones

Words and music by Babs Bell Hajdusiewicz

©1991–2011 Babs Bell Hajdusiewicz

My Faces (*anticipate*, 5s; *frantic*, 5s; *irritated*, 5s;
empathize, 7s)

I can make…
a funny face
a sunny face
a twitchy-nose-like-bunny face
a pouting face
a shouting face
a wondering-and-doubting face
a sad face

a mad face
a feeling-kinda-bad face
a scary face
a merry face
a what-a-sour-berry! face

Whatever face
You see in place
Is my how-I-am-feeling face!

Copyright © 1991 by Babs Bell Hajdusiewicz.
First published in *Poetry Works! The First Verse* by
Babs Bell Hajdusiewicz, Modern Curriculum Press/
PearsonLearning, 1993. See also *My Faces* above under
Picture Books, Early Readers, and Chapter Books.

My True Story (*exaggerate*, 4s; *observe*, 5s; *realistic*, 5s,
undoubtedly, 5s; *aghast*, 7s)

When I tell my true story to you,
you'll prob'ly say, "That can't be true!"

My head fell off the other day.
"That can't be true!"
My head fell off and rolled away.
"That can't be true!"
So I went shopping for a head.
"That can't be true!"
"We've lots of heads," the store clerk said.
"That can't be true!"
Then I picked out a head to buy.
"That can't be true!"
But that head's price was much too high!
"That can't be true!"
I headed home without a head.
"That can't be true!"
And there was my head–in my bed!
"That can't be true!"
My head began to squeal and scream!
"That can't be true!"
That noise woke me from my bad dream!
"That can be true!"

Copyright © 1991 by Babs Bell Hajdusiewicz.
First published in *Poetry Works! The First Verse* by Babs Bell
Hajdusiewicz, Modern Curriculum Press/PearsonLearning, 1993.

Nonfiction (*divulge*, 7s)
Nonfiction books are easy to find
With Dewey's system in my mind.
The number or subject is all I need
To find the book I want to read.

Copyright © 1992 Babs Bell Hajdusiewicz.
First published by Highsmith Upstart, Inc., 2005.

P—E—A—C—E (*undoubtedly*, 5s; *component*, 6s)

P—E—A—C—E
P—E—A—C—E
I make peace with my mouth.
I make peace with the words I speak.
I—make—peace!

P—E—A—C—E
P—E—A—C—E
I make peace with my hands.
I make peace with the things I do.
I—make—peace!

P—E—A—C—E
P—E—A—C—E
I make peace with my mouth.
I make peace with my hands.
I make peace!
I make peace!
'Cause I am Peaceful Me!

Copyright © 2007 Babs Bell Hajdusiewicz.

Babs Bell Hajdusiewicz

P-E-A-C-E!

© 2007 Babs Bell Hajdusiewicz

Rainbow Colors (*predict*, 4s)

Notes: Sing to the tune of "Twinkle Twinkle, Little Star"; North Africans refer to a rainbow as "bride of the rain," while Vietnamese call a rainbow "little window in the sky."

Red, orange, yellow
Green and blue
Indigo
And violet, too!

Bride of the rain
Little window in the sky
An arc of seven colors
When the sun is nearby!

Copyright © 1991 by Babs Bell Hajdusiewicz.
First published in *Poetry Works! The First Verse*
by Babs Bell Hajdusiewicz, Modern Curriculum Press/
PearsonLearning, 1992.

A Ruff Day (*perceive*, 6s)

I don't believe what I just saw—
Sam whacked Maggie in the jaw!
Maggie bit her brother's nose,
and Gigi pounced on Maggie's toes!
Then Elmer sneaked up—that's not kind!
He sank his teeth in Sam's behind!
And Maggie led the next attack
to land with Sam on Elmer's back!
Then Gigi sprawled atop the heap,
and all four puppies fell asleep!

Copyright © 1997 Babs Bell Hajdusiewicz.
From *Don't Go Out in Your Underwear!*
by Babs Bell Hajdusiewicz. Dominie Press/
PearsonLearning, 1997.

Skerbonker Doodles! (*bewildered*, 6s)

Skerbonker doodles!
These owies
And oodles
Of boo-boos kept coming my way!
Skerbonker doodles!
My owies
And oodles
Of boo-boos got bandaged today!

Copyright © 1992 by Babs Bell Hajdusiewicz
First published in *Poetry Works! The First Verse*
by Babs Bell Hajdusiewicz. Modern Curriculum
Press/PearsonLearning, 1992.

Sputter, Sputter, Sput! (*consume*, 5s)

I put some gas into my car.
Glug! Gurgle! Glug!
It makes my car go very far.
Zoom! Vroom! Zoom!
Uphill.
Downhill.
Up and down
past all the houses in my town.
But suddenly my car won't go!
Sputter! Sputter! Sput!
What's the matter?
I don't know.
Sputter! Sputter! Sput!
The other cars around me pass.
I think my car is out of gas.
I put more gas into my car.
Glug! Gurgle! Glug!
It makes my car go very far.
Zoom! Vroom! Zoom!
Uphill.
Downhill.
Up and down.
I drive my car—
right out of town.

Copyright © 2008 by Babs Bell Hajdusiewicz.
HarperCollins, 2008. See also *Sputter, Sputter, Sput!* above under
Picture Books, Early Readers, and Chapter Books.

Squirmy Earthworm (*positive*, 4s)

Note: A Fingerplay; sing to the tune of
"Itsy, Bitsy Spider" or sometimes called
"Eensy Weensy Spider"

Squirmy, Squirmy Earthworm
Lives down in the ground.
But watch her wiggle out
When rain falls all around!

Squirmy, Squirmy Earthworm
Squirms along the ground.
But watch her disappear when
Blackbirds come around!

Copyright © 1990 by Babs Bell Hajdusiewicz.
First published in *Poetry Works! The First Verse* by
Babs Bell Hajdusiewicz. Modern Curriculum Press/
PearsonLearning, 1992.
See also *Squirmy Earthworm* above under
Picture Books, Early Readers, and Chapter Books.

Standing Tall (*cautious*, 5s)

Note: Sing to the tune of "Are You Sleeping?"

I am standing.
I am standing.
Standing tall.
Standing tall.
Look how I am standing.
Look how I am standing.
I stand tall.
I stand tall.

Copyright © 2009 Babs Bell Hajdusiewicz.
From http://www.ilikeme.com/blog/?p=746.

A Stupid Feud (*ridiculous*, 4s)

Hugo and Buelah are feuding!
Hugo says Buelah won't share.
Buelah says Hugo refused to take turns...
Hugo says Buelah's not fair!

Their argument's lasted forever.
It's stupid!
They used to be friends.
If only they'd stop their ridiculous feuding.
I'm hoping their argument ends.

Copyright © 1998 Babs Bell Hajdusiewicz.
From *More! Phonics Through Poetry: Teaching Phonemic
Awareness Using Poetry* by Babs Bell Hajdusiewicz.
Good Year Books, 1999.

The Thinker (*ponder*, 6s)

His problem is surely a difficult one.
What can he be thinking about?
If I thought for more than four-hundred years,
I think I'd have figured it out.

Copyright © 1997 by Babs Bell Hajdusiewicz.
First published in *Don't Go Out in Your Underwear!*
by Babs Bell Hajdusiewicz. Dominie Press/PearsonLearning, 1997.

Who's the Boss? (*dominate*, 6s)

Who's the boss
of my tongue
and my hands
and my feet?
Who's the boss?
Who decides
how they'll act
when we meet?

I'm the boss
of my tongue
and my hands
and my feet.
I'm the boss!
I decide
how they'll act
when we meet!

Tongue Twisters/Alliterative Poems

Additional tongue twisters can be found in *Phonics Through Poetry: Teaching Phonemic Awareness Using Poetry* and *More! Phonics Through Poetry: Teaching Phonemic Awareness Using Poetry,* both by Babs Bell Hajdusiewicz, Good Year Books, 1999. See also http://www.fun-with-words.com/tongue_twisters.html.

Charlie's Chickens (*exceedingly*, 7s)

Charlie Chip was hungry
For some chunky chicken soup
So he went to choose a chicken
From his champion chicken coop.

But Charlie's champion chickens
Charmed poor Charlie with a chant,
"You can't make champions into chunks!
You can't!
You can't!
You can't!"

So Charlie Chip serves chitlins
With chilled chunks of cheddar cheese
While his charming champion chickens chant,
"Charlie, pass the peas!"

She Sells Sea Shells (*exceedingly*, 7s)

She sells sea shells by the sea shore.
The shells she sells are surely seashells.
So, if she sells sea shells by the seashore.
I'm sure she sells seashore shells.

Traditional Nursery Rhyme

Tricksters in Tales (*treacherous*, 7s)

Some tales tell of travels,
     and some tell of treasures.
And some tales of long, long ago
     tell stories of traitorous,
     troublesome tricksters
     whose actions caused troubles and woe:

One trickster, a wolf,
     tricked a trio of pigs—
     that traitor sought curly-tailed treats!
And one tricky trickster
     trapped children who trembled
     while nibbling a house trimmed in sweets.

One trickster, a shepherd,
     lost trust crying, "Wolf!"
     when a wolf wasn't trespassing there.
And tricksters entrusted
     to weave a king's trousers
     left one king tremendously bare!

In many a tale of long, long ago,
     untrustworthy tricksters
     caused troubles and woe.
But tricksters don't always
     know who is a friend,
     so… some tricky tricksters
     get tricked in the end!

INDEXES

Alphabetical Index

Index by Age

Games
(see Sports and Recreation)

Health and Safety

Home and Family

Imagination

Letters (see Numbers and Letters)

Manners and Behavior

Math (see Numbers and Letters)

Me

Music

Nonfiction

Shapes and Sizes

Sharing

Sizes (see Shapes and Sizes)

Sorting

Spatial Relationships

Sports and Recreation
(see also Play)

Surveys

Time

Transportation

Values

1, 2, 3. *consecutive*, 7s,   132

A clock is an advantage, *advantage*, 6s,   92

A diligent worker, *diligent*, 7s,   133

A T-rex bone—, *colossal*, 7s,   130

Accumulate books, *accumulate*, 7s,   127

An ominous look is all it took., *ominous*, 7s,   143

Appropriate is what appropriate does, *appropriate*, 5s,   53

At contribution time, *contribute*, 4s,   17

Cars consume their gasoline., *consume*, 5s,   59

Consider how terribly kind I am., *consider*, 4s,   16

Did Humpty Dumpty fall off the wall?, *positive*, 4s,   37

Don't tell me I can't do it., *discourage*, 5s,   61

Each remarkable sound, *remarkable*, 5s,   78

Earth's giving us oodles of cues, *conserve*, 5s,   58

Everyone called me Curious George, *curious*, 4s,   18

He doesn't fret., *nonchalant*, 7s,   142

He observed it all, *observe*, 5s,   71

He says he intends to be polite., *intention*, 6s,   108

Here's my perception, *perceive*, 6s,   114

His capacity for yelling, *capacity*, 6s,   98

His reasons seem transparent, *transparent*, 7s,   158

I adapt., *adapt*, 6s,   91

I am fairly flexible., *flexible*, 5s,   65

I am a prolific talker., *prolific*, 7s,   148

I could rule the galaxy!, *realistic*, 5s,   76

I do lots of things, *numerous*, 4s,   34

I don't know how to do it, *authority*, 5s,   55

I feel an obligation, *obligation*, 5s,   70

I feel enthusiastic! Rah-rah-rah!, *enthusiastic*, 5s,   63

I felt so aggravated, *aggravate*, 6s,   93

I frequently work., *frequently*, 5s,   67

I get a variety of choices., *variety*, 5s,   85

I guess, expect, *anticipate*, 5s,   52

I have an inquisitive mind., *inquire*, 4s,   28

I hold it in my fingers, *expand*, 4s,   24

I like kind things I see him do., *personable*, 7s,   144

I like it when it's tranquil—, *tranquil*, 7s,   157

I love Mom, *mutual*, 6s,   112

I made an error., *error*, 5s,   64

I might have said, "No", *spontaneous*, 6s,   119

I predicted all of my blocks might fall, *predict*, 4s,   39

I propose you do it., *propose*, 4s,   40

I recommend you just eat two., *recommend*, 5s,   77

I resemble my mom., *resemble*, 5s,   79

I took things literally., *literally*, 6s,   111

I try to be accurate., *accurate*, 4s,   13

I value me., *valuable*, 4s,   46

I want the max., *maximum*, 4s,   31

I was astonished to see my dog, *astonished*, 5s,   54

I was fascinated, *fascinating*, 4s,   25

I was feeling frantic., *frantic*, 5s,   66

I was tired and worn out., *exhausted*, 4s,   23

I was vigorously trying, *vigor*, 7s,   161

I'd never divulge our secret., *divulge*, 7s,   134

If dogs could talk, *confine*, 6s,   102

If I reach out, *simultaneous*, 7s,   153

If there's something suspicious about it, *suspicious*, 4s,   43

If you're prone to share, *prone*, 7s,   149

I'll try to ignore it., *ignore*, 5s,   68

I'll yield the floor to you, I will., *yield*, 6s,   123

I'm a yellow traffic sign., *cautious*, 5s,   56

I'm assuming you'll be helpful., *assume*, 6s,   95

I'm competent in math, *competent*, 7s,   131

I'm conscious of chores, *conscious*, 6s,   103

I'm determined to be, *determined*, 4s,   19

I'm elated!, *elated*, 6s,   106

I'm summoned, *summon*, 6s,   120

I'm telling you I feel aghast., *aghast*, 7s,   128

I'm thrifty, thrifty, thrifty., *thrifty*, 6s,   121

Interruptions!, *interrupt*, 4s,   29

Is it pertinent here?, *pertinent*, 7s,   146

Index of Additional Poems and Songs

Index of Additional Poems and Songs by First Line

CPSIA information can be obtained at www.ICGtesting.com
Printed in the USA
BVOW06s1209020814

360813BV00003B/9/P